The One Who Knows God

Excerpts From The Writings Of

Clement of Alexandria

A Modern English Rendition
from the translation of William Wilson, M. A.

The One Who Knows God.
Copyright © 1990 by David W. Bercot. All rights reserved.
For information address Scroll Publishing Co.,
Rt. 19, Box 890, Tyler, Texas 75706. No written
permission is needed for quotations of 75 words or less.

ISBN: 092-4722-029

Library of Congress Catalog No. 89-064491
Cover illustration: © Robyn Miller, 1990
Cover design: Robyn Miller

Printed in the United States of America

Contents

About This Translation 1
Clement: Teacher Of Wisdom 3

Part One
How To Use Wealth

1 The Heavy Burden Of Wealth...9
2 Re-examining Jesus' Words To The Rich Man 13
3 If You Want To Be Perfect 18
4 Cleansing The Soul..24
5 Even The Rich Can Be Saved 28
6 Love: The Greatest Commandment...................................35
7 Gathering An Army Of The Downtrodden.....................41
8 True And False Repentance..45

Part Two
The Life Of The One Who Knows God

9 Bearing The Cross 55
10 Love Not The World..58
11 Sojourners 65
12 The Prayer Life Of One Who Knows God 69
13 Holiness: A Joint Project...76
14 To Know God Is To Become Like Him 81
15 You Cannot Know God Without Faith............................84
16 To Know God Is To Love Others 88
17 How To Be Made Into The Image Of God 92
18 Oaths And Lawsuits..99
19 Christian Perfection...103
20 Women Who Know God 106
21 Searching For Truth...110
22 Scripture: The Basis Of Truth 113
23 Medicine For The Soul..118
24 Caring For Your Neighbor..123
   Appendix..126
   Index 133

About This Translation

Next to the Bible, the writings of the early Christians (90-325 A.D.) are the most valuable documents of Christianity. Like the Bible, they are part of the heritage of all Christians. Although these writings are not inspired, Scroll Publishing Co. believes that any translation of them should be undertaken as carefully as that of the Scriptures.

To that end, our contemporary renditions have been taken from the scholarly, careful translations that comprise *The Ante-Nicene Christian Library*. These translations were first published in 1867, in Edinburgh, Scotland, under the editorial supervision of Alexander Roberts, D.D., and James Donaldson, LL.D. As expressed by those editors, their objective was "to place the English reader as nearly as possible on a footing of equality with those who are able to read the original. With this view they [the translators] have for the most part leaned towards literal exactness; and wherever any considerable departure from this has been made, a verbatim rendering has been given at the foot of the page" (from the Preface to *The Ante-Nicene Christian Library*).

It was precisely this "literal exactness" that persuaded us to use the translations of Clement of Alexandria made by William Wilson, M. A., for *The Ante-Nicene Christian Library* as the basis for this work. We see little value in publishing a version of the early Christian writings that has been colored by the interpretations and theological biases of the translator. On the other hand, although we applaud the "literal exactness" of the *Ante-Nicene* translations, we realize that their stilted, archaic language discourages the modern layperson from reading them.

Therefore, the goal of Scroll Publishing is to render the early Christian works into contemporary, readable English while preserving the meaning of the original writers. To this end, we have followed a two-tiered system in our renditions:

We have been very strict in rendering passages containing material of theological, ecclesiastical, or moral significance to the modern reader. In such passages, we have aimed at "literal exactness," concentrating on faithfully communicating the writer's actual words or phraseology. We have not deleted any material from such passages.

However, we have paraphrased those passages that do *not* contain anything of theological, ecclesiastical, or moral significance to the modern reader. In such passages, we have concentrated on capturing as exactly as possible the meaning of the original writer, using simpler, more contemporary language. In such non-doctrinal passages, we have sometimes deleted sentences or clauses that are repetitious or whose meaning is obscure. However, all such deleted material has been reprinted in the appendix at the back of the book.

Our rendition, *The One Who Knows God*, is composed of two parts. Part One contains all of a tract or sermon by Clement of Alexandria entitled *Who Is The Rich Man That Shall Be Saved?* This work is arguably Clement's finest, and is certainly his most readable work. In it, Clement argues that the greatest treasure of all is to know God. Part Two of our rendition contains excerpts from Clement's work generally known by its shortened title, *Miscellanies*. This title is quite appropriate, for throughout this lengthy work (originally composed of eight books), Clement continually jumps from subject to subject. However, one theme that flows loosely throughout the work is the real meaning of knowing God. We have selected those chapters from *Miscellanies* that pertain to this theme. The appendix correlates the chapters herein with those of Clement's works.

To enhance the flow of both of these works, the modern editor has occasionally added transitional sentences between chapters. Such sentences, which do not appear in the original text, are designated with a printer's cross.[†] The modern editor has also furnished all chapter titles, subheadings, footnotes, and Scripture citations. There were no citations in the original texts. In fact, the Scriptures had not yet been divided into chapters and verses when Clement wrote these works.

The persons who rendered these writings of Clement into contemporary English (from the more literal translation of William Wilson) were Jeleta Eckheart, Beth Dillon Miller, and Pamela Warren. Jeleta Eckheart is an accomplished journalist who has edited several Christian books and periodicals. She obtained her Bachelor of Arts degree in literature and journalism with highest honors from George Washington University. Beth Dillon Miller studied at the Sorbonne in Paris, France, and obtained her B. A. summa cum laude from Xavier University. Pamela Warren is a gifted staff writer with Youth With A Mission, having served with this missionary organization since 1973.

The editor of this edition has been David W. Bercot. He obtained his Bachelor of Arts degree summa cum laude from Stephen F. Austin University and his Doctor of Jurisprudence degree cum laude from Baylor University School of Law. The early Christian writings have been his special field of study for a number of years. He is the author of the book, *Will The Real Heretics Please Stand Up*, which concerns the early Christians. He has also written articles for various journals about the early church.

Clement: Teacher Of Wisdom

In every age of man, there have been seekers of truth. In the second century, one such man was Titus Flavius Clemens, known better today as Clement of Alexandria. Although born to pagan parents, Clement realized that there must be a deeper meaning to life than the mundane pursuit of material riches and sensual pleasures. He heard about men who renounced the ordinary pursuits of life in order to seek after truth. These men were called philosophers, which means 'lovers of wisdom.'

So Clement studied the works of all the great philosophers who had lived before him, including the writings of thinkers from faraway lands such as Persia. From studying the works of these men, Clement learned that there was one true God who was above all the gods and goddesses worshipped by people of his day. He also learned that there was a more satisfying way of life than that sought after by most people. From his years of study, Clement came to be one of the most learned men of his day. Yet, he sensed that the philosophers had only knocked on the door of truth—that there was still greater truth that they had never discovered. When he finally heard the gospel of Jesus Christ, he knew this was the great truth he had been seeking all of his life.

After his conversion, Clement traveled throughout the ancient world to learn Christianity firsthand from the most respected teachers of his age—men who taught by deeds, not just words. Clement eventually settled in Alexandria, Egypt, where he served as an elder. In recognition of Clement's gift of teaching, the church of Alexandria appointed him as the instructor of new Christians.

The Works Of Clement

If you could have sat at the feet of Clement as a new Christian, what would you have learned? The chapters that follow are a collection of Clement's godly insights on the Christian life. In these chapters, he discusses prayer, the proper use of wealth, the life of holiness, separation from the world, marriage, love, women of wisdom, and the secret of tapping into God's power.

Part One of this book is a rendition of what was apparently a sermon or short tract of Clement, entitled *Who Is The Rich Man That Shall Be Saved?* This short work is the most eloquent and readable of all of Clement's writings. In it, Clement discusses Jesus' words to the rich young man, as recorded in Mark 10:17-31, sentence by sentence. His refreshing insights show that Jesus' words are addressed to each one of us, regardless of how much wealth we have.

Part Two contains selected chapters from Clement's longest work, known as the *Miscellanies* or *Patchwork*. The title could not be more appropriate, as this work is a loose amalgamation of Clement's thoughts on a variety of subjects, both spiritual and scientific. As one scholar put it, "Clement has the happy faculty of rarely sticking to the point. At the sight of the smallest hare running across the landscape, Clement is immediately after it."[1] Rather than following Clement as he 'chases those hares,' we have selected for this rendition only those chapters following the theme of what it really means to know God.

Clement firmly believed that the author of all truth is God. He also believed that God had planted seeds of truth in every nation of men. So unlike most Christians of his time, Clement had no qualms about quoting bits of poetry and passages of wisdom from the secular poets, writers, and philosophers. However, it is a mistake to think that Clement formulated his Christian beliefs from those sources. He himself described Greek philosophy as having only "a slender spark, capable of being fanned into flame, a trace of wisdom."[2] He also noted that it was "destitute of strength to perform the commandments of the Lord."³ As the chapters that follow will show, Clement was a man of the Bible. His beliefs came from Scripture and from the oral understandings handed down by the apostles—not from philosophy.

Clement wrote his *Miscellanies* around 190 A.D. At that time, the major heresy confronting the church was Gnosticism. The Gnostics claimed to have special knowledge (Gr. *gnosis*) about God, either through special revelation or through secret knowledge handed down by the apostles. Among other things, they taught that the God of the Old Testament was a different person than the God of the New Testament. They also taught that the Son of God had never really become human. (2 John 7-11)

In his *Miscellanies*, Clement attacked their claims by describing the lifestyle and prayer life of one who truly knows God (i.e. a true "gnostic"). He argued that those who deny or twist the Scriptures are not really "gnostics," for they have not come to know God in truth.

Through his spoken and written words, and by his godly lifestyle, Clement discipled hundreds of Christians. He led them into a life of undying love for God and fellowman, following in the footprints of Jesus. Among his noted students were Origen, the foremost Christian teacher in the third century, and Alexander, who became the overseer of the church at Jerusalem.

After Clement's death, his writings continued to instruct and inspire men and women of God through the centuries. The fifth century church historian, Theodoret, wrote about Clement, "He surpassed all others, and was a holy man."[4] Jerome said that he was "the most learned of all the ancients."[5] Even John Wesley was influenced by Clement's works. A more recent scholar wrote about him, "He read voluminously—there are more than 700 quotations from more than 300 authors in his works. ...He was gentle and considerate to all people, and was particularly understanding of women and children."[6]

Neither Catholic Nor Protestant

In most areas, Clement's works are very typical of early Christian thought. As you read his words, you will probably feel reassured that the early Christians believed many of the same things you do. At the same time, you will undoubtedly notice some views and practices that are different from your own. This is virtually everyone's experience upon reading the writings of the early Christians for the first time.

Actually, the early Christians do not fit perfectly into any of the denominational boxes of today. They are neither Catholic nor Protestant, liberal nor evangelical, charismatic nor fundamentalist. Yet, they have things in common with all of these groups. They bear witness to what Christianity was before it was stained by centuries of doctrinal disputes, complex theology, and denominational divisions. They reflect a Christianity that was known by its genuine love, simple holiness, and willingness to carry the cross.

---

[1] Robert Payne, *The Holy Fire* (New York: Harper & Rowe, 1957), p. 27

[2] Clement, *Miscellanies* bk. 1, chap. 17.

[3] *Ibid.*, chap. 16.

[4] Alexander Roberts and James Donaldson, "Introductory Note To Clement of Alexandria," in *The Ante-Nicene Fathers*, 10 vols. (Grand Rapids: Wm. B. Eerdmans Publishing Company, 1983), 2:166.

[5] *Ibid*

[6] Payne, p 25

Part One

How To Use Wealth

1

The Heavy Burden Of Wealth

Those who offer praises to rich people seem to me to be appropriately thought of as dishonorable flatterers. Not only do they vehemently pretend that disagreeable things give them pleasure, but they are godless and treacherous as well. They are godless because they fail to praise and glorify God. He is the only perfect and good one, "of whom are all things, and by whom are all things, and for whom are all things." (Rom. 11:36) They also bestow divine honors on mere men, who are wallowing in an abominable life. The most important thing is that they are responsible before God in this matter.

Those who praise the rich are really treacherous. By its very self, wealth is able to puff up and corrupt the wealthy. It thereby turns them away from the path by which they could obtain salvation. So when people praise the rich, they only compound the problem of wealth. They puff up the rich with their extravagant praise, thereby dulling their senses to the danger of wealth. The result is that the rich begin to utterly despise everything except wealth, for wealth brings them admiration. This only adds fire to fire and pours pride upon pride. It adds conceit to

> *By its very nature, wealth is a burden.*

wealth, making wealth an even heavier burden than it already is. For by its very nature, wealth is a burden. Its possessors would be better off if they would remove it as though it were a dangerous and deadly disease. For God's word teaches that anyone who exalts and magnifies himself will eventually be brought low. (Prov. 16:18)

It seems to me, then, that instead of basely flattering the rich and praising them for what is bad, it would be far kinder to help them work out their salvation in every possible way. We ought to ask for this salvation from God, who surely and sweetly gives such things to his own children. That way, by the grace of the Savior, we can enlighten the rich, lead them to attain the truth, and bring healing to their souls. Whoever obtains this salvation and distinguishes himself in good works will gain the prize of everlasting life. Prayer that continues until the last day of life needs a strong and tranquil soul. And our lives need to be ordered so that we can reach out [to obey] all the commandments of the Savior.

There are several reasons why salvation appears to be more difficult for the rich than for the poor. First, some rich people have heard it told, in an off-hand way, that the Savior said that "it is easier for a camel to go through the eye of a needle than for a rich man to enter into the kingdom of heaven." (Matt. 19:24) Having heard this, they despair that they are not destined to live. So they surrender everything to the world and cling to the present life as though it were the only thing left for them. This only takes them farther from the way that leads to the life to come. They don't bother to try to find out who the Lord and Master meant when he referred to the "rich." Nor do they discover that what is impossible for man is possible for God.

Other rich people adequately understand these things, but they don't give enough importance to the works that lead to salvation, and they don't make the preparation necessary to attain the object of their hope. But salvation is possible for the rich who have learned about the Savior's power and his glorious salvation. (I'm not addressing those who are ignorant of the truth.)

How To Assist The Rich To Salvation

If you would teach the truth about these matters to the wealthy, you must first be motivated by love of truth and love for your brothers. You must be neither rudely insolent toward the rich nor fawn over them for your own selfish benefit.

The next step is to relieve the rich of their groundless despair. This can be done by correctly explaining the Lord's statements, demonstrating that the rich are not entirely cut off from inheriting the kingdom of heaven if they obey the commandments. You must convince them that there is no cause for their fear, because the Lord will gladly receive them, provided they are willing. Finally, you must teach and demonstrate the deeds and attitudes by which they will win the object of their hope. It is not out of their reach, but it cannot be attained without effort.

To illustrate, look at athletes. (To compare something small and perishing with something that's great and immortal.) As with athletes, the man who is endowed with worldly wealth must realize that his obtaining the prize depends on himself. Among athletes, some give up hope of being able to win the trophy and drop out. Others are inspired by the hope of winning, but they fail to submit themselves to the necessary training, diet and exercises. So they likewise walk away without the trophy, failing to obtain their expectations.

In the same way, the man who has been invested with worldly wealth should not decide at the outset that he is excluded from the Savior's contest. That is, if he is a believer and he appreciates the greatness of God's mercy. On the other hand, he shouldn't expect to grasp the trophies of immortality without struggle and effort, remaining untrained and putting forth no effort. He must put himself under the Word as his trainer and submit to Christ as Master of the contest. His regimen of food and drink is the New Testament of the Lord. His training exercises are the commandments. For form and grace, he has the pleasant qualities of love, faith, hope, knowledge of the truth, gentleness, meekness, mercy, and seriousness.

In this way, when the last trumpet sounds the signal for the race and for his departure from the stadium of life, he will be able, in good conscience, to present himself victorious before the Judge who confers the rewards. He will be worthy of the Fatherland on high to which he returns with crowns, to the acclaim of the angels.

2

Re-Examining Jesus' Words To The Rich Man

Having begun the subject from this point, my prayer is that the Savior will allow me to share with these brothers what is true, what is suitable, and what leads to salvation. I first want to awaken in them the hope itself of eternal life. Then, I want to show them the access to that hope. Jesus gives to those who beg [for understanding], and he teaches those who ask. He makes ignorance vanish, and he dispels fear. His own words about the rich become their own interpreters and infallible expounders.

There is nothing like listening again to Jesus' own words—which until now distressed you when you heard them read from the Gospels. You who are wealthy were distressed because you heard them without examining them, and your immaturity led to an erroneous understanding of them. It is written:

> As they walked along, a man approached and kneeled, saying, "Good Master, what good thing shall I do that I may inherit eternal life?" Jesus said, "Why do you call me good? No one is good except God. You know the commandments. Do not commit adultery. Do not kill. Do not steal. Do not give false testimony. Do not defraud. Honor your father and your mother."

He answered him and said, "I have observed all these things." Jesus, looking at him, loved him, and said, "You still lack one thing. If you want to be perfect, sell what you have and give to the poor, and you will have treasure in heaven. And come, follow me." The man was sad about what he heard. He went away grieved, because he was rich, and he had many possessions.

Jesus looked around him and said to his disciples, "How difficult it is for those who have riches to enter into the kingdom of God! It is easier for a camel to enter through the eye of a needle than for a rich man to enter the kingdom of God." They were astonished beyond measure, and said, "Then who can be saved?" Looking at them, Jesus said, "What is impossible with men is possible with God. For with God all things are possible."

Peter began to say to him, "See, we have left everything and followed you." Jesus answered and said, "I tell you the truth, whoever leaves what is his own—parents, brothers and possessions—for my sake and the sake of the Gospel, will receive a hundred times as much, now in this world, of lands and possessions and houses and brothers, with persecutions. And in the world to come, he will receive life everlasting. But many who are first will be last, and the last will be first." (Mark 10:17- 31)

These things are written in the Gospel according to Mark. They're also written in all the rest [of the Gospels] in a similar manner. Although the expressions vary slightly in each book, they all agree identically in meaning.

We know that the Savior teaches nothing in a merely human way. Instead, he teaches everything to his followers with divine and mystic wisdom. So, we must not listen to his statements in a mundane, human sense. Instead, through appropriate investigation and intelligence, we must search out the real meaning hidden in his words. The things that the Lord himself seems to have simplified for the sake of the disciples are found to require not *less*, but *more*, attention than what is expressed through parables. That's because the seemingly simple statements are packed with such profound wisdom.

Moreover, the things that we think Jesus explained to the insiders—those he called the children of the kingdom—require even more consideration than the things that seem to have been expressed simply. The reason is that none of his listeners asked for a further explanation of such things. But since his words pertain to the entire design of salvation, we must contemplate these words with an admirable and heavenly depth of mind. We must not receive these statements superficially, with our *ears* only. Our *minds* must be attuned to the very spirit of the Savior and to the meaning *he* intended.

The rich young man pleasantly posed an appropriate question to our Lord and Savior. The question was appropriate because he asked Life itself about life. He asked the Savior about salvation, the Teacher about the primary teachings, and the Truth about true immortality. He addressed the Word about the word of the Father, the Perfect One about the perfect rest, and the Immortal One about true immortality.

By asking about eternal life, the young man addressed the very reason Jesus came to earth. He asked about the things Jesus taught and about the things he instilled in the minds of his disciples. In other words, he asked about the very essence of the Gospel. Being truly Divine, Jesus foreknew both what he would be asked and how each person would answer him. For who would be more capable of doing so than the Prophet of prophets, the Lord of every prophetic spirit?

> *The primary lesson for life is to know the eternal God.*

Having been called "good," he used this term as his starting point. In doing so, he turned his student to God, *the* Good, the first and only dispenser of eternal life. The Son, who received this eternal life from him, gives it to us.

Knowing God

The primary lesson for life must be implanted in the soul from the beginning. That lesson is to know the eternal God, the one who gives what is eternal. We can possess God through knowledge and understanding. He is the first and highest. He is one, and he is the [ultimate] good. This knowledge of God is the unchangeable and immovable source and support of life. He is the One who really is, and he gives the things that really are. That is, he gives the things that are eternal. The beginning of life—and the continuance of life—come from him. To continue to be also comes from him. Ignorance of him is death. For the only true life is this: to know him and take him for your own—to love him and to become like him.

Therefore, the man who wants to live the true life must first know the One that "no one knows, unless the Son reveals him." (Matt.11:27) Next, after Him, he must learn about the greatness of the Savior and about the newness of grace. For, according to the apostle, "the Law was given by Moses; grace and truth came by Jesus Christ." (John 1:17) The gifts granted through a faithful servant [Moses] are not equal to those given by the true Son. If the Law of Moses had been sufficient to give us eternal life, then there wouldn't have been any reason for the Savior to come and suffer for us. There would have been no need for him to follow the path of human life from his birth to the cross.

There also would have been no reason for the rich young man, the man who had followed all of the commandments of the Law from the time he was young, to fall on his knees and beg for immortality from another person. Notice that he had not only fulfilled the Law, but had done so since he was a very young boy. It doesn't surprise us if an old man is free of shortcomings. But when a carefree young man in the fire of his youth shows judgment beyond his years, this is a true champion. This is a man who is seasoned in mind, although young in body.

Re-Examining Jesus' Words To The Rich Man — Page 17

Nevertheless, because this rich young man was so wise, he knew that he was entirely destitute of real life, even though he lacked nothing in regard to righteousness. So, he asked for life from the only one who is able to give it. He was confident of his standing under the Law. But he approached the Son of God with humble petition. So, he was transferred from "faith to faith." (Rom. 1:17) It was as though he was on a storm-tossed sea, anchored only to the Law. So he headed for the Savior to find a safe haven.

In response, Jesus did not tell him that he had failed to fulfill all of the requirements of the Law. Instead, Jesus loved him and fondly welcomed his obedience as to the things he had learned. Then Jesus told the young man that he was not perfect with respect to eternal life. For he had not fulfilled what is perfect. He was indeed a doer of the Law, but he was idle at the *true life*. To be sure, the Law is good. Who denies that? For "the commandment is holy." (Rom. 7:12) It offers a sort of training with fear and preparatory discipline. In this way it leads us to grace and to the fulfillment of the Law. (Gal. 3:24) But Christ is the fulfillment of the Law for righteousness to everyone who believes. Christ is not a slave who is merely producing more slaves. Instead, he is producing sons, brothers and fellow-heirs, all of whom perform the Father's will.

3

If You Want To Be Perfect...

Ponder for a minute Jesus' words, "If you want to be perfect...." (Matt. 19:21) These words make it clear that the rich young man was not yet perfect. For there's no such thing as being *more* perfect. Notice also the divine expression, "if you wish to...." (Matt. 19:21) This shows that the young man's soul had the power of free will. Being free, the *choice* depended on the man himself. But the *gift* depended on God, who is the Lord. And God gives to those who are both willing and exceptionally earnest. That way, their salvation becomes their own. For God does not compel anyone [to come to him]. Compulsion is repugnant to him. Rather, he supplies to those who seek. He gives to those who ask. He opens to those who knock. (Matt. 7:7,8)

"If you want"—that is, if you *really* want and are not just deceiving yourself—then obtain what you lack. "One thing you are lacking,"—the one thing that endures. It is the good thing that is above the Law. The Law cannot give this and it cannot contain it. This one thing is the prerogative of those who really live. This young man had fulfilled all the requirements of the Law from the time of his youth. He had gloried in what was magnificent. Yet, he was not able to complete [his quest] by adding the one thing that the Savior particularly required. He was unable to receive the eternal life he so desired. So he went away distressed, upset at the one commandment of [eternal] life that he had asked about.

What was his problem?* His problem was that he did not *really* desire life, as he claimed. All he wanted was the *reputation* of seeking the good. He was quite capable of busying himself with all sorts of things. But he was powerless when it came to the work of life. The Lord had spoken similarly to Martha. She was busy with many activities, distracted and troubled with serving. And she criticized her sister for leaving the work of serving in order to sit at Jesus' feet and devote her time to learning. As Jesus told Martha, "You are troubled about many things, but Mary has chosen the good part, and it will not be taken away from her." (Luke 10:41,42) In the same way, the Lord told the rich young man to leave his busy life and cling to the grace of the one who offered everlasting life.

Is It Wrong To Own Possessions?

Why, then, did the young man leave the Master? Why did he so quickly abandon the life and hope he had been so earnestly pursuing? It was because Jesus told him, "Sell your possessions." But what did Jesus mean? Jesus was *not* saying, as some people quickly conclude, that the young man should throw away all he owned and abandon his property. Instead, the Savior was directing him to banish from *his soul* all his views about wealth—both his excitement and his worries. He directed him to abandon his material anxieties, which are the thorns of existence that choke the seeds of life. (Matt. 13:22)

After all, it is no great thing to simply be destitute, unless there's a special purpose behind it. That purpose must be life! Otherwise, the only ones to possess eternal life would be those who beg for their daily bread, even though they know neither God nor his righteousness. And the persons most blessed and dear to God would be those who have nothing at all—the poor who wander the streets—even though they don't know God. The destitute would have eternal life simply because of their extreme want and their lack of material things.

Furthermore, remember that renouncing one's wealth and giving it to the poor was no new thing. Many people had done this before the Savior came to earth. Some people [like the philosophers] did it in order to pursue empty human wisdom. Still others, like Anaxagoras, Democritus and Crates did it for empty fame and the praise of men.*

Why, then, did the Master command it as though it were something new and divine—as though it alone were life-giving? After all, this very same thing did not save people in times past. So what was this special thing the Son of God was teaching? It was not the outward act—the thing that many others had already done. Rather, it was something greater, more godlike, and more perfect: *To strip the desires of the flesh from one's very soul.* To pull up from the roots and throw away the things that are alien to the soul [or mind]. This is the instruction worthy to come from the Savior himself. This is the teaching that is unique to believers.

In the past, those who renounced external things gave up only their material possessions. But at the same time I think they *intensified* the longings of the flesh. For they were arrogant, pretentious, and boastfully vain. They treated the rest of mankind with contempt and acted as though they had done something superhuman. Why would the Savior have told the very people who were destined to live forever that they should do what would be harmful to the very life he promised? After all, a person may get rid of the burden of wealth and still have his innate lust for money. He may abandon what he has—only to long for what he once had. So, he will grieve twice as much. Most certainly, those who lack the necessities of life will be mentally anguished. In trying to somehow provide for their needs, they will be hindered from better things.

The Proper Use Of Wealth

How much better it is for a man to have some possessions so he can keep himself out of dire straits and so he can give

---

*These three men were Greek philosophers who lived centuries before Christ.

assistance to those who require it! If no one had anything, how could we give to others? Isn't it clear that a literal interpretation of Jesus' words contradicts many of his other teachings? For example, Jesus said, "Make friends with the riches of unrighteousness, so that when you fail, they may welcome you into the eternal dwellings." (Luke 16:9) He also said, "Acquire treasures in heaven, where moths and rust cannot destroy them, and thieves cannot break in." (Matt. 6:20) Jesus taught that we must give food to the hungry, drink to the thirsty, clothing to the naked, shelter to the homeless, or else be punished in fire and outer darkness. (Matt. 25:31-46) But how could a person do these things if he has divested himself of all his goods?

No, in fact, the Savior once invited Zaccheus and Matthew, the rich tax collectors, to entertain him hospitably. (Luke 5:29) He didn't require *them* to part with their property. Instead, he applied just judgment to them, saying [about Zaccheus], "Today, salvation has come to this house, because this man is also a son of Abraham." (Luke 19:9)

In fact, Jesus has so much praise for the appropriate use of wealth that he orders that it be shared, in order to give drink to the thirsty, bread to the hungry, shelter to the homeless and clothing to the naked. It's not possible for a man to provide those needs unless he has material possessions of his own. So if the Lord was really calling people to abandon all of their material possessions, he would have been telling us both to give and not to give at the same time. He would be telling us to feed and not to feed. To take in and shut out. To share and not to share. That would be most irrational!

So, riches that benefit our neighbors as well as ourselves are not to be thrown away. They are appropriately called "possessions," since they are possessed. They are called "goods," since they are useful and provided by God for the use of men. They are under our control. And they are an instrument for good use to those who know how to use the instrument. If you use it skillfully, it is skillful. If you are unskilled, it's affected by *your* lack of skill. In itself, it is not to be blamed. Are you able to make a right use of wealth? Then it will be a servant to righteousness. Do you use it wrongly? Then it is a minister of wrong. Its nature is to serve, not to rule.

Therefore, the thing that has no good or evil in and of itself should not be blamed. The one who should be blamed is the one who chooses to use it either for right or for wrong purposes. The responsible party is the mind and judgment of man. Man has the liberty and free will to determine how he will use what is assigned to him. So, let no man destroy wealth when he should be destroying the fleshly desires of the soul. For these desires are incompatible with the better use of wealth. By destroying these desires, a person becomes virtuous and good. He is thereby able to make a good use of his riches. In summary, the renunciation of riches and the selling of all possessions refers to the fleshly desires of the soul.

Some things are inside the soul and some things are outside of it. If the soul makes good use of something, it is deemed to be good. But if the soul makes bad use of something, it is deemed to be bad. So, when Jesus commanded us to alienate our possessions, was he speaking about the *physical things* that can be cast away while the fleshly longings [for material things] still remain? Or was he speaking about the *materialistic desires*, which once removed, allow wealth to even become beneficial?

So the man who casts away his worldly wealth can still be rich in materialistic desires, even though he has no money to gratify his desires. So, it is of no advantage to him to be poor in purse if he is still rich in materialistic desires. He has cast away the wrong thing—something that is neither good nor evil by itself. At the same time, he has deprived himself of something serviceable. And, he has set the inborn fuel of evil on fire because he has no means to satisfy his material lusts.

> *The man who casts away wealth can still be rich in materialistic desires.*

Therefore, we must renounce only those things that are injurious—not those that can be of service when they are used properly. Whatever is managed with wisdom, sobriety and godliness is profitable. But whatever is harmful must be thrown out. However, external things of themselves cannot hurt us. So then, the Lord introduces the proper use of external things. He does not tell us to put away our means of livelihood. Rather, he tells us to put away the sickness and materialistic desires of the soul. These cause us to use our wealth in a harmful way.

4

Cleansing The Soul

Anyone who combines wealth with wrong desires has mixed a deadly combination. In such a case, to lose the wealth would be a healthy alternative. To make the soul pure—that is, poor and bare—we need to focus on the next words of the Savior, "Come, follow me." (Mark 10:21) He becomes the way to the pure in heart. God's grace finds no entrance into the impure soul. And the soul that is rich in desires, entangled with affection for the things of the world, is impure.

Yet, some people are able to hold their gold, silver, houses, and other possessions simply as the gifts of God. They use their things to minister for the salvation of men. They thereby return them to God, who gave them. They know that they possess them more for the sake of their brothers than for themselves. They are the *masters* of their belongings, not the *slaves* of their possessions. They don't carry their belongings around in their *soul*, nor do they plan their life around their things. Instead, they are always laboring at some good, divinely-inspired activity.

Even if they sometimes need to be deprived of their things, they are able to cheerfully bear the removal of their belongings just as easily as they were able to enjoy their abundance. (Phil. 4:11,12) These are the ones who are blessed by the Lord. They are the ones he calls "poor *in spirit*." (Matt. 5:3) They are the proper heirs of the kingdom of heaven.

But there are others who carry their riches *in their soul*. Instead of being filled with God's Spirit, their hearts are filled with their gold or their land. They are always acquiring possessions, and they are perpetually on the lookout for more. They are bent down and fettered to the toils of the world. They are of the earth and destined to become a part of the earth. How can they desire or pay attention to the kingdom of heaven? They don't carry around *hearts* in their bodies. Instead, they carry around land or precious metals. You'll always find them in the midst of the objects they have chosen. For where the mind of man is, there also is his treasure. (Matt. 6:21)

The Lord says that there are two kinds of treasures. First, there's the good kind: "The good man, out of the good treasure of his heart, brings forth good." (Matt. 12:35) And then there's the evil kind: "The evil man, out of the evil treasure, brings forth evil, for the mouth speaks out of the abundance of the heart." (Matt. 12:34,35) So according to Christ, there are two different kinds of treasure, the kind that gives an unexpected great gain when you find it, and the kind that is profitless, undesirable, and even harmful. So there is a richness in good things and a richness in bad things. It is appropriate to possess and acquire the first sort of riches, but the other kind should be cast away.

Genuine And Counterfeit Poverty

In the same way, spiritual poverty is blessed. That's why Matthew added, "Blessed are the poor." (Matt. 5:3) What kind of poor? Those poor *in spirit*. In the same way, he says, "Blessed are those who hunger and thirst after the righteousness of God." (Matt. 5:6) How wretched indeed, then, are the other type of poor—those having no part in God and even less in human property. These are the ones who have not tasted the righteousness of God.

So, the expression, "How difficult it is for those who have riches to enter into the kingdom of God," must be taken with careful thought, rather than in a clumsy or fleshly way. When the expression is understood the right way, it is clear that salvation does not depend on external things—whether there be many or few, small or large, shiny or dull, valuable or cheap. Rather, salvation depends upon the virtues of the soul—faith, hope, love, brotherhood, knowledge, meekness, humility, and truth. The reward for these is salvation.

Likewise, no one is granted life on account of his physical beauty. Nor is anyone doomed to perish because he is not handsome. But anyone who uses the body he's been given in a chaste manner and according to God's design, will live. And anyone who destroys God's temple will be destroyed. (1 Cor. 3:16) After all, an ugly man may be immoral, and a handsome man may be self-controlled.

Likewise, the strength and size of the body do not give life. Nor do any members of the body destroy life. But the soul, which uses the body, provides the cause for either life or destruction. To illustrate, we are told that when we are struck on the face, we should simply endure it. (Matt. 5:39) A strong and healthy man is capable of obeying this command, [even though his body could enable him to strike back]. And a poor and feeble man may just as easily break this commandment because of his nasty temper. In the same way, a poor and destitute man may be drunk with the desire for material goods, while a man rich in worldly goods may be sympathetic and pure. He may exercise self-control and only rarely indulge himself.

> *The one who is truly rich is the one who is rich in virtue.*

So the soul is the first and most important aspect of our living. The virtue that springs up in the soul is what saves. And corruption [of the soul] kills. So let's stop looking for the cause of life and death anywhere else other than in the soul's purity and obedience to God. Or, the soul's breaking of the commandments and its accumulation of wicked behavior.

So, the one who is truly rich is the one who is rich in virtue. He is able to use his fortune in a faithful and holy way. On the other hand, the one who is falsely rich is the one who is rich only according to the flesh. He turns life into a matter of outward possession, which is transitory and perishing. Today it may belong to one person, tomorrow to another. And in the end it belongs to no one at all.

In the same way, there is a genuine poor man and a counterfeit poor man. To be poor *in spirit* is the right thing. To be poor in a worldly sense is a different matter. To the one who is poor in worldly goods but rich in vices, it is said, "Abandon the alien possessions that are in your soul, so that, by becoming pure in heart, you may see God." To put it another way, "Enter into the kingdom of heaven." For such a person is not poor in spirit and rich toward God.

How do you abandon those possessions? By selling them. But then what? Should you exchange your personal effects for money, simply changing your riches from one form into another? Not at all. Instead, you should dispose of it in accordance with the command of God. You do that by bringing into your soul the kinds of riches that deify and that minister everlasting life. By doing so, the following things will accrue to you: endless reward and honor, salvation, and everlasting immortality. That is the right way to sell your belongings. Your many superfluous possessions shut the heavens against you. But you may exchange them for those that are able to save. Let those who are poor in a carnal sense have your possessions. They are destitute of the things that save. But you, by receiving spiritual wealth instead, will now have treasure in the heavens.

5

Even The Rich Can Be Saved

The rich young man, who was righteous according to the Law, did not understand the things Jesus said figuratively. He could not see how the same person could be both poor and rich. How he could both *have* wealth and *not* have it. How he could use the world and not use it. So he went away sad and downcast. He walked away from the life that he desired but could not obtain. In this way, he turned something that was *difficult* into something that was *impossible*.

To be sure, it's difficult for the soul not to be seduced and ruined by the luxuries and enchantments that come with great wealth. But it's not *impossible*—even for those who are surrounded by wealth—to lay hold of salvation. It's not impossible, that is, if such a person withdraws his attention from the wealth that is material and turns it instead to the wealth that only the mind can grasp—the wealth taught by God. Such a person must learn to properly use material things (which are indifferent to good or evil), and he must strive after eternal life.

Why The Apostles Were Alarmed

Notice that at first, even the disciples were alarmed and amazed [by what Jesus told the young man]. Why? Was it because they themselves were wealthy? Definitely not. They had already left their nets, hooks and rowing boats—their sole possessions—long before this time. Why, then, did they ask with dismay, "Who can be saved?" (Mark 10:26)

The reason was that, as good disciples, they had understood what the Lord was figuratively saying. They perceived the *depth* of his words. Up to that point, they had been confident of their own salvation on the grounds that they were not wealthy. But when they realized that they had not yet fully renounced their *materialistic desires*, they were distressed. Remember, they were neophytes, only recently selected by the Savior. So they were as much in despair about their own condition as was the rich young man who clung so fiercely to the wealth that he preferred more than eternal life.

And they had good reason to fear. Both the person who possesses wealth and the one who is teeming with materialistic desires are "the rich." And the rich will be expelled from the heavens. For salvation is the privilege of pure souls free from fleshly desires.

Salvation: A Joint Project

But the Lord answered their despair by saying, "What is impossible with men is possible with God." (Mark 10:27) Once again, his words were full of great wisdom. A man working by himself to gain freedom from his fleshly desires achieves nothing. But if he plainly shows himself to earnestly desire this freedom, God will give him the power to attain it. God conspires with willing souls. But if they abandon their eagerness, the Spirit who is bestowed by God will be restrained. For to save those who are unwilling is the role of one who exercises compulsion. But to save those who are willing is the role of one who shows grace.

> *The kingdom of heaven does not belong to sleepers and lazy people.*

The kingdom of heaven does not belong to sleepers and lazy people, "but the violent take it by force." (Matt. 11:12) This is the only commendable kind of violence: to force God, and take life from God by force. He knows who perseveres firmly (or violently), and he yields and grants to them. For God delights to be conquered in this way.

Upon hearing Jesus' words, blessed Peter—the chosen, the preeminent, the first of the disciples, and the only one for whom the Savior ever paid taxes (other than himself)—immediately grasped the sense of them. (Matt. 17:27) Notice his reply: "We have left everything and followed you." (Mark 10:28) Now if all he meant was that he had left his own property, he boasted of leaving only about four oboli [2/3 of a drachma] in all.* And he would have been forgetting to acknowledge that the kingdom of heaven was their reward for leaving behind such a small amount of property.

But if he was talking about leaving what I was previously discussing—the old mental possessions and soul diseases—for the purpose of following in the Master's footsteps, then, by this act, they joined the others who are to be enrolled in the heavens. For to truly follow the Savior is this: To aim at sinlessness and His perfection, to adorn and compose the soul before the mirror of Christ's perfection, and to arrange everything in our lives to reflect that image.

Jesus continued his instruction by saying, "I tell you the truth, whoever leaves what is his own—parents, and children, and wealth—for my sake and for the sake of the Gospel, will receive a hundred times as much." (Mark 10:29, 30) But don't be troubled by that saying, nor by one that is even harder: "Whoever does not hate his father, and mother, and children, and his own life besides, cannot be my disciple." (Luke 14:26) The God of peace, who exhorts us to love even our enemies, obviously doesn't want us to hate our dear ones and dissolve our relationships with them. If we are supposed to hate our relatives, we should hate our enemies even that much more. Simple logic tells us that. But that would contradict Jesus' teachings.

---

*A drachma was the daily wage of a laborer.

Instead, Jesus' commands do not contradict each other. However, in applying Jesus' words, a person who loves his enemy may also "hate" his father. That's because he neither takes vengeance on his enemy, nor venerates his father more than Christ. The first command ['love your enemy'], destroys hatred and injury. The second command ['hate your father'], prevents excessive attachment toward your relatives, when such behavior is detrimental to salvation. In other words, if someone's father, or son, or brother, is godless, and if they become a hindrance to the believer's faith and an impediment to the higher life, then the believer should not be friends with them or agree with them. Because of the spiritual enmity, he should dissolve the fleshly relationship.

For example, suppose there's a lawsuit. Imagine that your father presents himself to you and says, "I brought you into being and I raised you. Join me in wickedness, and do not obey the law of Christ." And suppose he says other things that a blaspheming man with a dead nature would say.

On the other side, hear the Savior saying, "You were born into the world, headed for death. But I gave you new life. I freed, healed, and ransomed you. I will show you the face of the good Father, God. Do not call any man on earth your father. Let the dead bury the dead, but you follow me. (Matt. 23:9; 8:22) I will bring you to a rest of overwhelming, indescribable blessings, which eye has not seen, nor ear heard. It has not even entered into the heart of men. Angels long to look and see what good things God has prepared for the saints and the children who love him. (1 Cor. 2:9; 1 Pet. 1:12) I am the one who feeds you. I give you myself as bread. Anyone who tastes this bread no longer experiences death. (John 6:51) And I supply, day by day, the drink of immortality. I am the teacher of heavenly lessons. For you, I struggled with death. And I paid *your* death, which you owed for your former sins and your unbelief toward God."

Having heard the arguments on both sides, decide for yourself. Cast your vote for your own salvation. Even if your brother made the same claims, or your child, or your wife—or anyone else. In preference to all of them, let Christ be the conqueror in you. For he fights on your behalf.

You may say to yourself, "Certainly Christ does not prevent me from owning property. The Lord does not envy [my possessions]." That's true.† But are you overcome and conquered by your wealth? If so, leave it. Throw it away. Hate it. Renounce it. Flee from it. As Jesus said, "Even if your right eye offends you," quickly "cut it out." (Matt. 5:9) The kingdom of God is better to a man with one eye than the fire is to someone who is unmutilated. Whether it's your hand, your foot, or your soul [that offends you], hate it. For if it is destroyed in this life for Christ's sake, it will be restored in the life over there.

Our Savior continued his instructions to his disciples, talking about leaving lands, money, houses and brothers in this life—but receiving more, with persecutions. It's not particularly the penniless, the homeless, and those who don't have a family that the Lord invites to eternal life. As we have shown above, he has also called rich people. And he also called brothers, such as Peter and Andrew, or James and John, the sons of Zebedee. But they were of one mind with each other and with Christ.

The Two Kinds of Persecution

Then what about the expression "with persecutions"? By this, he means that we must not grasp at money, property and family. You see, there are two kinds of persecutions. One kind comes from the outside. It comes from men who attack God's faithful people, because of hatred, envy, greed, or demonic pressure. But the most painful kind of persecution is that which is internal. This persecution comes from each person's own soul, as the soul is plagued by irreverent lusts, diverse pleasures, earthly hopes, and destructive dreams. It is always grasping for more. Maddened by savage loves, it is inflamed by the passions that attack it like stinging insects. It is covered with blood that drives it on to insane pursuits. In the end, it

> *The most painful kind of persecution is that which is internal.*

leads a person to give up hope for [eternal] life, and to have contempt for God.

Internal persecution is more painful because it is always with a person. The persecuted one cannot escape it, because he carries the enemy everywhere inside himself. The persecution that comes from outside is merely a trial. But what comes from inside produces death. The war from without may be easily ended, but the internal war in our souls continues until the day we die.

So, in light of this persecution, abandon whatever leads you to evil—whether it be your worldly wealth or your fleshly brothers and other pledges. Instead, procure peace for yourself by freeing yourself from these prolonged persecutions. Turn from them to the gospel. Above everything else, choose the Savior and Advocate and Paraclete of your soul, the Prince of life. "For the things that are seen are temporary; but the things that are not seen are eternal." (2 Cor. 4:18) In the present life, everything is vanishing and insecure. But what is to come is eternal life.

[Jesus concluded by saying], "The first will be last, and the last first." (Mark 10:31) This saying is full of meaning, but it doesn't demand immediate investigation. For it doesn't refer only to the wealthy, but to all men who have surrendered themselves to faith. So let this stand aside for the present.

I think I have demonstrated my premise as I promised I would. That is, the Savior has by no means excluded the rich from eternal life on account of their wealth. Nor has he fenced off salvation from them because they possess property. But they must be able and willing to submit their lives to God's commandments. They must prefer his commands to the transitory objects of this life. And they must look to the Lord with a steady eye, like those who look for the nod of a good helmsman. They must see what he wishes, what he orders, and what he indicates. They must see what signal he gives his mariners and where he directs the ship's course.

But what harm has anyone done, if, before he became a believer, he applied his mind, saved his earnings, and collected a sufficient means for his needs? And it is certainly less reprehensible if, by God—who gives each one his life—someone has been born into a home among people who are wealthy, powerful, and influential. If a man were banished from [eternal] life simply because he was involuntarily born into wealth, then he would be wronged by God. For God, who created him, would have given him temporary enjoyment only to deprive him of eternal life. In fact, why should wealth have ever sprung from the earth, if it is the author and patron of death?

But what if someone is able, although in the midst of wealth, to turn away from its power? What if he is still able to maintain moderation in his feelings and to exercise self-control? What if he is able to seek God alone—to breathe God and walk with God? Then such a man is really poor. He submits to God's commandments and he is unconquered and unharmed by wealth. He lives free of its disease. But if that's not the case, then "it will be easier for a camel to go through a needle's eye, than for such a rich man to reach the kingdom of God." (Mark 10:25)

Now I will present the point of this parable of the rich young man and explain why it is told. Its purpose is to teach the prosperous that they are not to neglect their own salvation, thinking that they are already destined to face doom. Nor should they cast their wealth into the sea or condemn it as a traitor and an enemy to life. Instead, they must learn how to use wealth and obtain life. Certainly, no one perishes [simply] because he frets over the fact that he is rich. Likewise, no one is saved [simply] by trusting and believing that he will be saved. Instead, people should investigate the hope that the Savior gives them. By investigation, they should find out how they can confirm that which is unexpected. They can thereby possess the thing they hope for.

6

Love: The Greatest Commandment

When he was asked, "Which is the greatest of the commandments?" the Master said, "Love the Lord your God with all your soul and with all your strength." (Matt 22:36-38) He said that no commandment is greater than this, and he said so with good reason. For this is a command about our behavior toward the first and the greatest—God himself. He is our Father. He is the one who has brought all things into being, and everything exists through him. Everything that is saved returns to him. He has loved us beforehand, and we receive our existence through him. Therefore, it is irreverent for us to regard anything else as being older or more excellent than him.

We are required to deliver only this small tribute of gratitude [our love] for the great benefits God gives us. In fact, I cannot imagine any other way to repay God, who needs nothing and is perfect. Yet we gain immortality by the very fact of our loving the Father to the fullest extent of our might and power. Because the more we love God, the more we enter within God.

The second commandment he mentioned, which is no less important, is to "Love your neighbor as yourself." (Matt. 22:39). Please note, that you are to love God *above* yourself. So someone asked Jesus, "Who is my neighbor?" (Luke 10:29) He did not answer the way the Jews would have. They would have said their neighbors were their blood relatives. Or their fellow citizens, or the proselytes. Or perhaps those who had been circumcised in the same way, or the people who followed their Law.

Instead, the Master talked about a man on his way down from Jerusalem to Jericho. Robbers stabbed the man and left him half dead on the road. A priest passed him by, and a Levite merely gave him a sideways glance. Only the maligned, outcast Samaritan had pity on him. Rather than casually passing by like the others, the Samaritan provided what the man in danger needed—oil, bandages, a beast of burden, and money for the innkeeper (part given in advance, and part promised).

"Which of them," Jesus asked, "was a neighbor to the man who suffered?" His listener answered, "The one who showed mercy to him." The Master replied, "So you should go and do the same thing," since love blossoms into benevolence. (Luke 10:36,37)

So, in both commandments, Jesus focused on love. But he distinguished their order. He assigned the foremost part of our love to God and the second part to our neighbor. Who is the Samaritan who has shown love for us other than the Savior himself? Who has pitied us more than he has? The rulers of darkness had all but put us to death with wounds, fears, lusts, passions, pains, deceits, and pleasures. Jesus is the only physician for these wounds. He cuts out our fleshly desires thoroughly—by the root. The Law only cuts out the bare effects—the fruit that grows on our evil plant. But Jesus applies his ax to the *roots* of our wickedness.

Like the Samaritan,† Jesus is the one who has poured wine (the blood of David's vine) onto our wounded souls. He is the one who has brought the oil that flows from the Father's compassion and poured it freely on our wounds. He is the surgeon who has sewed us up with those threads of health and salvation that cannot come loose—love, faith and hope. He is the one who has subjected angels, principalities and powers to serve us, as his reward to us. For they will also be delivered from the vanity of the world through the revelation of the glory of the sons of God.

Therefore, we are to love Jesus equally with God. And the one who loves Christ Jesus is the one who does his will and keeps his commandments. He said, "Not everyone who says to me, 'Lord, Lord' will enter the kingdom of heaven—only he who does the will of my Father." (Matt. 7:21) And he said, "Why do you call me 'Lord, Lord' when you don't do the things that I say?" (Luke 6:46) And "blessed are you who see and hear what neither righteous men nor prophets" [have seen or heard], if you do what I say. (Matt. 13:16,17)

So first is he who loves Christ. But next is he who loves and cares for those who have believed in Christ. For when you do something for a disciple, the Lord treats it as though you did it to him. He will say, "'Come, you who are blessed by my Father, inherit the kingdom prepared for you since the foundation of the world. For I was hungry, and you gave me something to eat. I was thirsty, and you gave me something to drink. I was a stranger, and you took me in. I was naked, and you clothed me. I was sick, and you visited me. I was in prison, and you came to me.' Then the righteous people will answer, saying, 'Lord, when did we see you hungry and feed you, or thirsty and give you something to drink? And when did we see you a stranger and take you in? Or naked and clothe you? Or when did we see you sick and visit you? Or in prison and come to you?' And the King will answer and say to them, 'I tell you truly, in the same way that you have done it to the least of these my brothers, you have done it to me.'" (Matt. 25:34-40)

> *The one who loves Christ Jesus is the one who keeps his commandments.*

On the other hand, to those who have not shown kindness in this way, [he will say], "I tell you truly, since you have not done it to the least of these my brothers, you have not done it to me." (Matt. 25:45) Similarly, in another place it is recorded that he said, "He who receives you, receives me. And he who does not receive you, rejects me." (Matt. 10:40; Luke 10:16)

Making Friends With Unrighteous Riches

These are the people he calls his little children, his sons, and his friends. When he does so, he refers to their future greatness above. He says, "Do not despise one of these little ones, for their angels always behold the face of my Father in heaven." (Matt 18:10) In another place, he says, "Do not be afraid, little flock, for it is your Father's good pleasure to give you the kingdom of heaven." (Luke 12:32) In the same way, he also says that the least person in the kingdom of heaven who is his disciple is greater than John, who was the greatest man born of women. (Matt. 11:11) And again he said, "Anyone who receives a righteous man or a prophet will receive his reward, and anyone who gives a cup of cold water to a disciple in the name of a disciple will not lose his reward." (Matt. 10:42) This is the only reward that cannot be lost.

He also said, "Make friends with the wealth of unrighteousness, so that when you fail, they may receive you into eternal homes." (Luke 16:9) When he said this, he showed that by its nature, all property that a man possesses by his own power is not really his own. And from this unrighteousness [i.e. wealth], we are allowed to perform a righteous and saving thing—to refresh those who have an eternal dwelling with the Father.

Notice that he has not told you to wait until someone asks or begs you to share your wealth. No. You yourself must look for those worthy disciples of the Savior whom you can aid. As the apostle has most excellently put it, "The Lord loves a cheerful giver." (2 Cor. 9:7) The cheerful giver delights in giving. He doesn't hold anything back. Instead, he sows so that he will reap. He does it without murmuring, disputing, or showing regret. This is giving that is pure. Even more blessed is what the Lord said in another place: "Give to everyone who asks you." (Luke 6:30) This shows how delighted God is when we give. And this saying is above all divinity: not waiting to be asked, but finding out for ourselves who deserve to receive kindness.

What a rich reward God promises us for our generous giving: an eternal dwelling place. What an excellent trade! What divine merchandise! We can purchase immortality with money. By giving up the perishing things of the world, we can receive in exchange an eternal mansion in the heavens. Sail to this market, if you are wise, rich man! If need be, sail around the whole world. Do not spare whatever perils and toils it takes, so that you may purchase the heavenly kingdom while you're still here. Why do transparent stones and emeralds delight you so much? Why get so excited about a house that is only fuel for a fire, or a plaything of time, or the sport of an earthquake, or the plunder of a tyrant's fury?

Aspire to dwell in the heavens and reign with God! A mere man who is imitating God may give you a kingdom *here on earth*. But by receiving only a little here, God will make you a dweller there with Him through all ages. Ask that you may receive. Hurry! Strive! Fear lest he disgraces you. For God is not commanded to receive, but you are commanded to give. The Lord did not simply say, "Give, or bring, or do good, or help." Rather, he says, "Make a friend." A friend proves his friendship not simply by giving a single gift. Rather, he shows it by developing intimacy over a long period of time. For it is not the faith, love, hope, or endurance for just one day. But "he who endures *to the end* will be saved." (Matt. 10:22)

> *It is not the faith of just one day. But he who endures to the end will be saved.*

How then does man give? For I will give not only to friends, but to the friends of friends. And who is it that is the friend of God? Don't *you* judge who is worthy or unworthy. For it is possible that you will be mistaken in your opinion. It is better to do good to the undeserving for the sake of the deserving than to fail to meet the needs of the good because you are guarding against those who are undeserving. By holding back and testing whether someone is worthy or not, you may neglect someone God loves. And the penalty for that is the punishment of eternal fire. (Matt. 25:41-46) But if you offer to help anyone who has need, you will certainly find someone who has power with God to save. As Jesus said, "Don't judge, so that you will not be judged. With whatever measure you measure out, it will be measured back to you." And again, "A good measure, pressed and shaken together and running over will be given to you." (Matt. 7:1,2; Luke 6:37,38)

Open your compassion to all who are enrolled as the disciples of God. Don't look contemptuously at personal appearance. Don't be carelessly disposed to only a certain age group. If someone appears to be penniless, or ragged, or ugly, or feeble, don't let your soul fret about it and turn away from them. Our bodies are only a form cast around us. They are the occasion of our entrance into this world, and they allow us to enter into this common school. But inside of us dwells the hidden Father, and his Son, who died for us and rose with us.

7

Gathering An Army Of The Downtrodden

Actually our outward, visible appearance cheats death and the devil. For death and the devil don't see the wealth and beauty that are inside us. They rave about the carcass, which they despise as being weak. But they are blind to the wealth within. They don't know what a "treasure in an earthen vessel" we carry. (2 Cor. 4:7) This treasure is protected by the power of God the Father, and the blood of the Son of God, and the dew of the Holy Spirit. But you who have tasted of the truth and have been counted worthy of the great redemption must not be deceived. Unlike the armies of other men, you should collect for yourself an unarmed, peaceful, bloodless, restrained army: One of pious old men, orphans dear to God, widows armed with meekness, and men adorned with love. Use your money to gather these guards of your body and soul. For their sake, a sinking ship is buoyed, steered by the prayers of the saints alone. Disease at its height is put to flight by the laying on of hands. The attack of robbers is spoiled by righteous prayers. And the might of demons is crushed, vanquished by strenuous commands.

All of these warriors and guards are trusty. None of them are idle. Not one of them is useless. For one of them can obtain pardon from God for you. Another can comfort you when you're sick. One can weep and groan in sympathy for you to the Lord of all. Another can teach you some of the things that are useful for salvation. One can admonish you with confidence. Another can counsel you with kindness. And all of them can love you truly, without cunning, without fear, without hypocrisy, without flattery, without pretense. What sweet service comes from loving [souls]! What blessed thoughts come from confident [hearts]! What sincere faith belongs to those who fear God alone! What truthful words come from those who cannot lie! What beautiful deeds come from those who have been commissioned to serve, please, and plead with God.

All the faithful, then, are good and godlike. They are worthy of the name that circles their heads like a crown. But then there are also some people who are the elect of the elect. They are more distinguished because they draw themselves out of the surge of the world to safety, like a ship to its mooring. They don't wish to seem holy. In fact, they're embarrassed if anyone calls them such. (So in a sense, they are less distinguished.) They hide in the depths of their minds the inexpressible mysteries [of God]. They disdain to display their nobleness just to be seen by the world. They are the people the Word calls "the light of the world, and the salt of the earth." (Matt.5:13, 14)

These are the seed, the image, and the likeness of God. These are his true children and heirs. They were sent here on a journey by the arrangement and government of the Father. Both the visible and invisible things of the world were created by the Father. Some of these were sent for their service. Others, for their discipline. Still others, for their instruction. All things are held together as long as this seed remains here. But when the seed is gathered, these things will be very quickly dissolved.

God: The Loving Parent

What further need does God have for the mysteries of love? Some day you will look into the bosom of the Father—the One alone whom the Only-Begotten Divine Son has declared. (John 1:18) God himself is love. Out of his love for us, he became feminine. In his indescribable essence, he is Father; but in his compassion for us, he became Mother. By loving, the Father became feminine. The great proof of this fact is the One he begot out of himself. And the fruit brought forth by love is love.

Because of love, he [Jesus] came down to earth. Because of love, he clothed himself with man. For love, he voluntarily subjected himself to the experiences of men. He did this so that by bringing himself down to the weakness of those he loved, he could bring us up to the measure of his own strength. As he was about to be offered up as a ransom, he left us a new covenant-testament: "I give you my love." How great is that love? He gave his life for each of us—one life for all.

So now he demands that we give our lives for one another. Therefore, since we have made this mutual agreement with the Savior that we owe our lives to our brothers, why should we hoard our worldly goods any longer? After all, they are transitory, worthless, and foreign to us. Shall we lock up from each other what will be the property of the fire after a little while. John makes a divine and weighty statement when he says, "He who does not love his brother is a murderer." (1 John 3:15) He is the offspring of Cain, a nursling of the devil. He does not have God's compassion. He has no hope of better things. He is sterile. Barren. He is not a branch of the ever-living heavenly vine. He is cut off, waiting for the perpetual fire.

> *Now he demands that we give our lives for one another.*

Instead, learn the more excellent way. The one Paul points to for salvation, saying, "Love is not self-seeking." (1 Cor. 13:5) Rather, it is poured out on your brother. Love trembles over your brother and is soberly insane about him. "Love covers a multitude of sins." (1 Pet. 4:8) "Perfect love drives out fear." (1 John 4:18) Love "does not boast; it is not proud. Love does not delight in evil, but rejoices in the truth. Love bears all things, believes all things, hopes all things, endures all things. Love never fails. Prophecies are done away with, tongues cease, gifts of healing fail on the earth. But these three abide: faith, hope, and love. But the greatest of these is love." (1 Cor. 13:4-8,13)

That statement is true. For faith departs when we are convinced by vision, by seeing God. And hope vanishes when the things we hope for come. But love comes to completion, and grows even more, when that which is perfect has been given to us. If one brings love into his soul—although he has been born in sins, and has done many forbidden things—he is able to retrieve his mistakes by increasing love and by adopting a pure repentance.

8

True And False Repentance

If someone is able to escape the excesses of riches, and is able to overcome the difficulties that riches cause in the way of life, he can enjoy eternal good things. But suppose that even though he is sealed* and redeemed, for some reason—because he doesn't know any better or because of circumstances he cannot control—he falls into sins and is quite carried away. What happens? This person is entirely rejected by God.

Everyone who has turned to God with his whole heart will find that the doors are open. The Father gladly receives his truly repentant son. And true repentance is to be no longer bound in the same sins for which the Savior has denounced death against himself. Rather, it is to eradicate those sins completely from our souls. When those sins are pulled up by their roots, then God makes his home in you again.

It is said that the Father and the angels have great joy and celebration when one sinner turns and repents. (Luke 15:10) God tells us, "I prefer mercy, and not sacrifice." (Hos. 6:6; Matt. 9:13) And "I desire not the death, but the repentance of the sinner." (Ezek. 18:23) And he says, "Though your sins are like scarlet wool, I will make them as white as snow; though they are blacker than darkness, I will wash them and make

---

* "Sealing" refers to baptism.

them like white wool." (Isa. 1:18) Only God has the power to forgive our sins and pardon our transgressions. But he also commands us to daily forgive our brothers when they repent. (Matt. 6:14) "And if we, being evil, know how to give good gifts" (Luke 11:13), then how much more it is the nature of the long-suffering Father of mercy and consolation to wait for those who have converted. But to convert means that we really do cease from our sins, and we no longer look behind.

So, God is the one who forgives our past sins. But we forgive ourselves of future sins. We do this by repenting, by condemning the past deeds, and begging the Father to totally forget them. The Father is the only one who is able to undo what has been done and to blot out our former sins by the dew of the Spirit. He says, "I will judge you by the state in which I find you." So, there may be a person who has done incredibly good deeds during his life. But if he runs headlong into wickedness at the end of his life, then all his previous good deeds will fail to profit him. At the conclusion of the drama, he has given up his role.

> *True repentance is to be no longer bound in the same sins.*

On the other hand, it is possible for the man who once led a wicked and immoral life to eventually repent. During the remainder of his life after his repentance, he may overcome the evil conduct of a long time. But to do so requires great care, because he is like one who has suffered from a prolonged disease and needs to follow a certain regimen. He needs special attention. Thief, do you want to be forgiven? Steal no more. Adulterer, burn no more [with lust]. Fornicator, live purely in the future. You who have robbed, give back—and give back more than you took. False witness, practice truth. Perjurer, swear no more. All of you, get rid of the rest of your fleshly passions—wrath, lust, grief, fear. In doing so, at the end of your life, you may be found to have already been reconciled to the adversary during your stay in this world.

It is probably impossible to eradicate all your inbred passions at once. But by God's power, by human intercession, by the help of the brothers, by sincere repentance, and by constant care, they will be corrected.

Find Yourself A Mentor

Therefore, it is necessary for you who are pompous, powerful, and rich to find a man of God to set over yourself as a trainer and mentor. Have godly respect for someone—even if it's only for one man. Answer to someone—even if it's only to one man. Learn to listen to someone else, though there may be only one other man who speaks candidly to you. His words may be harsh, but they will bring healing. For your eyes should not continue unrestrained. It is good for them to sometimes weep and hurt. This will bring you greater health in the long run. Likewise, nothing is more detrimental to the soul than uninterrupted pleasure.

Learn to fear this godly man [i.e. your mentor] when he is angry. Be pained at his groaning. Respect him as you learn to put a stop to what causes his anger. Anticipate him when he is pleading against your punishment. Let him spend many sleepless nights out of concern for you, interceding with God for you, influencing the Father with the magic of his familiar prayers. For the Father does not hold out against his children when they beg for his pity. And your mentor will pray for you in a pure manner, held in high honor as an angel of God. He'll be grieved not *by* you, but *for* you. This is sincere repentance. "God is not mocked." (Gal. 6:7) Nor does he give heed to vain words. Only he can search the depths of our hearts. He hears those who are in the fire. He listens to those who pray from in the whale's belly. He is near to everyone who believes, but he's far from the ungodly if they do not repent.

A True Life Example Of Repentance

I want you to be even more confident that this kind of repentance brings you the certain hope of salvation. So I will tell you a story that has been handed down and committed to memory about the Apostle John.

When the tyrant [Domitian, who had exiled John] finally died, John left the island of Patmos and returned to Ephesus. He was then asked to travel throughout the surrounding provinces. In one place he would appoint overseers. In another, he would set whole churches in order. In still another, he would ordain those who were indicated by the Spirit.

Along the way, he stopped at one of the cities not far from Ephesus. Some have said this city was Smyrna. After he had settled some other matters, he noticed a strong, handsome young man who was enthusiastic and devoted. Looking at the newly-appointed overseer, he said, "I commit this youth to you in all earnestness, in the presence of the church, and with Christ as witness." When the overseer accepted the charge and promised to fulfill his obligation, John gave him instructions and testimony. Then John returned to Ephesus.

The elder took the youth who had been committed to him to his own home. He reared him, cherished him, and finally baptized him. After this, he relaxed his stricter care and guardianship. He thought that the seal of the Lord he had set on the youth [i.e. baptism] gave him complete protection. But when the youth obtained this premature freedom, some other young men his age, who were idle, immoral, and adept at evil, corrupted him. First, they enticed him by providing expensive entertainment. Later, when they went out at night and robbed people on the highways, they took him along. Then they dared to pull off bigger things. By degrees, he came to accept their life. He had a strong nature, so once he had left the right path, he was like a hard-mouthed and powerful horse. He had taken the bit between his teeth, and he rushed with all the more force down into the depths.

In time, he entirely despaired of salvation in God. He no longer desired to do small acts of evil—but great ones. Since he felt he was lost beyond all hope, he made up his mind to accept the same fate as the others. Taking them and forming a band of robbers, he quickly became the captain of the bandits—the fiercest, bloodiest, and cruelest of them all.

Time passed. Some necessity emerged in the church, so they sent for John to come to them again. When he had settled this other matter, John said, "Overseer, return the deposit which I and the Savior committed to you in the presence of the church over which you preside." At first, the overseer was puzzled, thinking John was wrongly accusing him of mishandling money. He couldn't believe the allegation, but neither could he disbelieve John. Finally John clarified the matter, saying, "I demand the young man, and the soul of our brother entrusted to you."

The elderly overseer, groaning deeply, burst into tears and said, "He is dead."

"How did he die?"

"He is dead," the overseer said, "to God. He turned wicked and abandoned the faith. And at last he became a robber. Now he and his band have taken possession of the mountain across from the church."

John tore his clothes and pounded his head with a great lament. "I left a fine guard in charge of this brother's soul!" he finally cried.

Recovering, he said, "Someone please bring me a horse. I need a guide to show me the way." He rode away, just as he was, straight from the church. As he approached the robbers' hideout, he was grabbed by their sentry. Neither fleeing nor begging, he cried out, "I came here so that you could waylay me. Lead me to your captain." Meanwhile, the captain, who was fully armed, was waiting. But as soon as he recognized John, he was overcome with shame. He quickly turned and fled. John followed him with all his strength, forgetting his age, and cried out, "Why, my son, do you flee from me, your old and unarmed father? Son, pity me. Do not fear. You still have hope of life. I will give an account to Christ for you. If need be, I will willingly endure your death, as the Lord endured death for us. For you I will surrender my life. Stop! Believe! Christ has sent me."

The youth finally stopped, and he stood looking down. He finally threw down his weapons. Then he trembled and began to weep bitterly. When the old man approached, he embraced him. Though the young man could hardly speak because he was crying so much, he expressed his regret for his actions. That day, he was baptized a second time with tears. But he still concealed his right hand.* John assured him on oath that he would find forgiveness from the Savior. Begging him and falling on his knees, John kissed his right hand, purified by repentance. Then he led him back to the church.

There John prayed profusely, striving beside the young man in continual fasting. Through hours of instruction, he subdued the young man's mind. In fact, John did not depart until he restored the young man to the church. He presented the young man as a great example of true repentance and a token of new birth. He was a trophy of the resurrection in which we hope. For at the end of the world, the angels, radiant with joy, singing hymns and opening the heavens, will receive those who truly repent into the celestial abodes. On that day, in front of everyone, the Savior himself will go to greet them and welcome them. Holding forth the eternal light that is without shadow, he will conduct them to the Father's bosom, to eternal life, to the kingdom of heaven.

> *If you turn away from the Savior, you can blame neither God, nor riches, nor the fallen flesh.*

So believe the prophecies, the gospels, and the apostolic words. By living in accordance with them, lending your ears, and practicing these deeds, when you die, you will see the fulfillment of these truths. For anyone who welcomes the angel of repentance in this world will not need to repent when he dies. He will not be ashamed when he sees the Savior approaching in his glory and with his army. He will not fear the fire.

On the other hand, if you choose to continue to sin perpetually in pleasures—if you prefer to indulge yourself here

---

*His right hand was his sword hand.

rather than to seek eternal life—if you turn away from the Savior who offers forgiveness—blame neither God, nor riches, nor the fallen flesh. Blame your own soul, which voluntarily perishes. For whoever desires salvation and asks for it vehemently and boldly, the good Father in heaven will grant true purification and the changeless life. To him, by his Son Jesus Christ, the Lord of the living and the dead, and by the Holy Spirit, be glory, honor, power, and eternal majesty, both now and forever, from generation to generation, and from eternity to eternity. Amen.

Part Two

The Life Of The One Who Knows God

9

Bearing The Cross

The one who knows God will follow the Lord's footsteps, bearing the cross of the Saviour. It is said, "The world is crucified to him, and he to the world." (Gal. 6:14) The Lord says, "He who loses his life will save it." (Matt. 10:39) We can "lose our lives" in one of two ways. First, we can risk our lives, just as the Lord did for us. Secondly, we can separate our lives from the customary things of this world. Bearing the cross means to separate our souls from the delights and pleasures of this life. If you do this, you will find your life again—resting in the hope of what is to come. Dying to ourselves means being content with the necessities of life. When we want more than these necessities, it is easy to sin.

"We must therefore put on the armor of God, to be able to stand against the schemes of the devil. The weapons of our warfare are not physical, but powerful through God to pull down strongholds, and cast down arguments and everything exalting itself against the knowledge of God. We must bring every thought into captivity to the obedience of Christ," says the divine apostle. (Eph. 6:11)

What is needed is a man who handles the circumstances of life in a discerning and praiseworthy manner. I'm speaking of the contrasting circumstances that may come our way. Such as riches and poverty. Honor and dishonor. Health and sickness. Life and death. And work and pleasure. The world sees a great difference between these contrasts. But the one who knows God views them all with indifference.

The Need For Endurance

Endurance is another godly trait. Daniel, who was filled with divine faith, was a good example of one who had endurance. He lived in Babylon, similar to the way that Lot lived in Sodom and that Abraham lived in Chaldea. (This Abraham was called the friend of God.) The Babylonian king threw Daniel into a pit of wild beasts, but the King of all, our faithful Lord, brought him out unharmed.

The one who knows God will have this same kind of patient endurance. When under trial, he will bless God like Job did. Like Jonah, he will pray when swallowed by a great fish. He will pray, and faith will bring him back to prophesy to the people of Nineveh. Though penned up with lions, he will tame them. Though cast into the fire, he will not be destroyed. Rather, he will be covered with dew. He will testify both day and night by his words, his conduct, and his very life. His best friend will be the Lord, and he will share the same hearth with the Spirit. He will be pure in the flesh, in his heart, and in his speech.

Spiritual Warfare

When we lived in the flesh, we were feeble. This was due, [in part], by our poor discipline. We used to indulge all of our desires without limit. However, now we recognize our fleshly desires as being imprints on our souls—imprints left by the wicked spirit forces with whom we struggle. The powers of evil try to leave their mark on everything they touch. They thereby try to win back those who have renounced them. As might be expected, these evil powers re-conquer some.

However, others of us enter the struggle against them with more athletic energy, so to speak. (I'm using the terms of the public games by way of illustration.) The evil powers attack the faithful with every weapon they have, locking arms in bloody combat. But eventually the evil powers have to give up the battle. They retreat with admiration for the victorious Christian.

We humans have the faculty of reason. Therefore, we should not be carried away by mere appearances. Rather, we should look beyond them. The powers of evil hold out beautiful sights to humans, such as worldly honors, adulteries, fleshly pleasures, and similar alluring fantasies. They try to lure men the way a herdsman leads cattle with food. They deceive those who can't tell the difference between true and false pleasure. Or between fading beauty and that which is holy. Having deceived such people, they lead them into slavery. Each false allurement leaves its imprint on the spirit by constantly pressing against it. By our falling for the bait, our soul unwittingly carries about the imprint of our fleshly desires.

> *The powers of evil try to lure men the way a herdsman leads cattle with food.*

10

Love Not The World

The one who knows God has the same attitude towards both body and soul. He treats all persons alike—whether they are his neighbors, his servants, or his legally-declared enemies. He does not despise his brother, who according to the divine law, is of the same father and mother. He helps those in need by giving comfort and encouragement, and by providing the necessities of life. He gives to all who need. But he does so justly—according to what each one deserves. So the one who knows God grows to the point of knowing *to whom* he should primarily give, *how* he should give, *when* he should give, and *how much* he should give. The practice of giving liberally, which prevails among us, is properly called "righteousness." But the power of discerning who deserves what amount of assistance is a form of the very highest righteousness.

He even gives to the one who persecutes and hates Christians, if that person has need. He doesn't care if people think he is helping his persecutor out of fear. He knows that his motive is not fear, but is only to give help. So when we know God, we share our belongings with our enemies. We hate evil—even when it's done to our enemies. How much more so, then, are we filled with love for those who belong to us.

Who could become the enemy of a man who gives no cause for hatred in any way? Is not that how it is with God? We say that God treats no one as an enemy. For he is the Creator of all. And nothing that exists is what he wills it not to be.

Instead, we declare that those who are disobedient and who do not live by God's commandments treat God as an enemy. They are hostile to his covenant. So the one who knows God can never view or treat anyone as an enemy. Rather, those who follow a different path treat the man of God as an enemy.

Some people practice control over pleasures in a very crude way. They are like the pagans. For some pagans abstain from earthly delights simply because they have no way of obtaining them. Or because they fear what others will think. Or because they want even greater pleasures. Likewise, some believers exercise self-restraint only because of the promise of reward or out of fear of God. Of course, this kind of self-restraint is a start.† It's the basis of knowledge, and it's the first step towards something better. It's an effort after perfection. For it is said that "the fear of the Lord is the beginning of wisdom." (Prov. 1:7)

> We hate evil—even when it's done to our enemies.

But the *perfect* man "bears all things" and "endures all things" out of love. (1 Cor. 13:7) He does it "not to please man, but God." (1 Thess. 2:4) Although praise may follow him as a result, he does not do things to receive praise. He does them for the benefit of those who do the praising. He also does them to set an example for others.

To put it another way, the person who merely controls his *wrong* desires is not truly a moderate man. The true man of moderation is one who has also mastered good attributes. He has acquired the great things that come from knowledge. He produces godly qualities as the fruit of this knowledge. The one who knows God is never dislodged from his way of life, even in an emergency. The good he possesses through knowledge is firm and unchangeable. For he has the knowledge of things both divine and human. This type of knowledge can never turn into ignorance, any more than good can turn into evil.

The one who knows God eats, drinks, and marries, not as ends in themselves, but simply as necessary things. I include marriage in this list only to the extent the Word dictates and only as it is suitable. For having become perfect, the one who knows God has the apostles as examples. One is not really proven to be a man by the choice of the single life. But the one who has been disciplined by marriage, the raising of children, and the care of his household surpasses other men. When he cares for his household without pleasure or pain, he becomes inseparable from God's love. For he has withstood all temptations arising through children, wife, servants, and possessions. But he that has no family is free of temptation to a large degree.

But, to the extent possible, we must subject the soul to various disciplines so it will be more open to receive knowledge. For example, wax first has to be softened before it can be imprinted with a stamp. Likewise, copper has to be purified before it can be imprinted.

Death is the separation of the soul from the body. Likewise, knowledge is a sort of death caused by reason. It separates the spirit from the desires of the flesh. And it leads the spirit into a life of doing good, so that the spirit can say with confidence to God, "I live as you want me to." He who makes it his purpose to please men cannot please God. For the crowd does not choose what is profitable, but what is pleasant. But when we please God, we also win the favor of good people.

> *It is impossible for the one who truly knows God to serve pleasures that oppose God.*

How can the things concerning meat, drink, and passionate pleasure be compatible with a man of God? He is suspicious of anything that stimulates fleshly pleasure: a word, a pleasant movement, or a thought. "For no one can serve two masters, God and Mammon," it is said. (Matt. 6:24) Mammon refers not simply to money, but to the pleasures money can buy. In reality, it is impossible for the one who truly knows God to serve pleasures that oppose God.

There is only one who was free of immoderate desire his whole life. That was the benevolent Lord, who became man for us. Whoever tries to receive the stamp imprinted by him must strive to be free of immoderate desires. And this takes practice. The one who has fallen to immoderate desires, but thereafter restrains himself, is like a widow who becomes a virgin again by celibacy. (1Tim. 5:9,10) Such is the reward of knowledge: refraining from evil and doing what is good, by which salvation is acquired. These things are rendered to the Savior and the Teacher, as he himself has asked.

People make a living doing what they have been taught. In the same way, the one who knows God is saved, obtaining life by what he knows. But he who does not desire to completely uproot the sinful desires of the soul kills himself. So it seems that ignorance starves the soul and knowledge sustains it.

Prayer Life

The souls of those who know God are likened by the gospel to the consecrated virgins who wait for the Lord. (Matt. 25:1-13) They are virgins in the sense of refraining from what is evil. They wait out of love for the Lord, and they light their lamps in expectation of the things to come. They are wise souls, saying, "Lord, we have long desired to receive you. We have lived by what you have counseled, disobeying none of your commandments. So we also claim your promises. And we pray for what is beneficial since it is not necessary to ask of you what is most excellent. We shall view everything you bring us as being good. This is so even though the trials we face, which you bring on us to train us in steadfastness, may appear evil."

When a person knows God, his whole life is prayer and conversation with God. If he is pure from sins, he will certainly obtain what he wishes. God says to the righteous man, "Ask, and I will give to you. Think, and I will do." If what he asks is beneficial, he will receive it at once. If it is harmful, he will never ask for it. So he will not receive it. In this way, it shall be as he wishes.

However, someone may say, "Even some sinners get what they request." My reply is that this rarely takes place, because of God's righteousness and goodness. But God answers those people who are capable of doing good to others. So the gift is not given for the sake of the one who asked. Instead, God gives it because he foresees that someone will be saved because of it. So the gift is still given for a righteous purpose. Truly good things are given to those who are worthy, even without their asking.

Whenever a person is righteous by free choice—not from necessity, or fear, or hope [of reward]—this is called the royal road. For the royal people travel it. Other roads are slippery and steep. For example, look at the most famous of the philosophers, who speak so boldly. If the motives of fear and fame were removed, I doubt they would be willing to endure hardships any longer.

Working For God

Lusts and other sins are called "briars and thorns." (Matt. 13:7) So the one who knows God labors in the Lord's vineyard. He plants, prunes, and waters. He is the divine gardener of what is planted in faith. Those who have simply abstained from evil deeds think they deserve the wages of ease. But he who has done good deeds out of free choice demands his pay as a good workman. He shall certainly receive double wages. God will reward him both for the good he has done and for the evil he has not done.

The one who knows God is not tempted by anyone except with God's permission. Then it would be for the benefit of those who are with him. He strengthens them for faith, encouraging them by brave endurance. Surely the apostles were brought to trial and martyrdom for this same reason. By their sufferings, they established and confirmed the churches.

The one who knows God hears a voice ringing in his ear, saying, "You should have compassion on the ones I plan to punish." He pleads so that such persons will repent, even though they hate him. For the public punishment of criminals along the highways is not even for children to witness. The one who knows God, who has trained himself in righteousness, cannot enjoy or learn from the punishment of his enemies. He is unable to be softened by pleasures, and he never falls into sin. So he is not corrected by the examples of other men's sufferings. He has shown a noble contempt for the rewards held out in this world. So he receives no enjoyment at all from earthly pleasures and entertainment.

"Not every one who says 'Lord, Lord,' shall enter into the kingdom of God, but he who does the will of God." (Matt. 7:21) This is the laborer who knows God. He has mastered worldly desires while still in the flesh. He regards the unseen future to be more real than the earthly things around him. This competent workman rejoices in what he knows. Still, he feels cramped because of having to take care of life's necessities. So he uses this life as if it belonged to another.

Fasting

He understands the real purpose of fasting on Wednesday and Friday.* His very life is a fast—a fast from envy and sensuousness. For all sins stem from those. The one who knows God fasts 'according to the Law' by abstaining from evil *deeds*. He fasts 'according to the perfection of the Gospel' by abstaining from evil *thoughts*. As I have said, temptations are brought before him, not for his purification, but for the good of his neighbors. He treats trials of labor and pain with disdain, passing them by.

> His very life is a fast—a fast from envy and sensuousness.

The same is true of pleasure. When someone has been tested by fleshly pleasures, it is a supreme achievement for him to abstain from pleasure. What great thing is it if a man restrains himself when he is not tempted? So according to the

---

*Literally, the Fourth and Preparation.

gospel, a person keeps the Lord's day when he abandons an evil nature and when he takes on the nature of one who knows God. He thereby glorifies the Lord's resurrection in himself. When he understands through knowledge, he feels as though he has seen the Lord. Of course, he still sees the evil things of this world with his literal eyes, even though he would rather not. But he directs his eyes towards invisible things. He disciplines his eyes when he realizes that he is enjoying the things his eyes see in this world. (1 John 2:15-17) For he would rather see and hear only those things which concern [eternity].

When he looks at the souls of his brothers [in Christ], he also sees the beauty of their flesh. For his soul has become accustomed to look solely upon that which is good, without carnal pleasure. They are truly his brothers, because God created them. Furthermore, they have the same character and the same deeds. They do, think, and speak the same holy and good works, endowed with the feelings that the Lord wishes the elect to be inspired with. A common faith is demonstrated by their choosing the same things. A common knowledge is demonstrated by their learning and thinking the same things. And a common hope is shown by their desiring the same things.

11

Sojourners

If, because of the necessities of life, the one who knows God must spend a small portion of time in providing sustenance, he feels cheated. For some of his attention is diverted by business. Not even in his dreams does he look on anything unsuitable to a chosen man. He is a complete stranger and sojourner on this earth. He lives in the city, but despises the things in the city which others admire. He lives in the city as though he were living in a desert. (Heb. 11:13-16)

In summary, the one who knows God makes up for the fact the apostles are no longer with us. His does this in several ways: By the uprightness of his life. By the accuracy of his knowledge. By taking care of his relatives. By helping his neighbors remove their mountains of doubt and by helping them put away the sins of their soul. Still, each of us is his own vineyard and laborer.*

Although he does the things that are most excellent things, he wishes to escape the notice of men. He would rather know before the Lord and himself that he is actually living in accordance with the commandments. He prefers these things because he truly believes them to exist. "For where anyone's mind is, there also is his treasure." (Matt. 6:21)

Through the perfection of love, he impoverishes himself so he will never overlook a brother in need. This is especially

---

*In other words, each of us must answer for himself.

so if he knows that he can bear want easier than his brother. He considers the other's pain his own grief. If he suffers any hardship by giving out of his poverty, he does not complain. Rather, he increases his generosity. For he possesses a sincere faith that is worked out in everyday life. He praises the Gospel both in thought and in deed. He truly wins his praise "not from men, but from God," by doing what the Lord has taught. (Rom. 2:29)

Drawn by his own hope, he does not taste the good things of this world. Instead, he has a noble contempt for all things here. He pities those who are chastised after death, who unwillingly make confession as a result of punishment. In contrast, he has a clear conscience as to his departure, and he is always ready for it. He is "a stranger and pilgrim" regarding earthly possessions. (1 Pet. 1:17) He is mindful only of those things that are his own. But he regards all earthly things as not his own.

> *He impoverishes himself so he will never overlook a brother in need.*

He not only delights in the Lord's commandments, but partakes of the divine will through knowledge. Because of his righteousness, he is truly a select, intimate friend of the Lord and of the Lord's commands. As one who knows God, he is both princely and kingly. He disdains all the gold on the earth and under the earth. And he disdains rulership from ocean shore to ocean shore. He disdains these things so he can cling to the Lord's service. So in eating, drinking, marriage (if the Word commands), and even his dreams, he does and thinks what is holy.

As a result, the one who knows God is always pure for prayer. He prays in the society of angels, for in a sense he is already of angelic rank. And he is never out of the holy keeping of the angels. Even though he prays alone, he has the choir of the saints standing with him.

He recognizes that there are two elements [in faith]. First, there is the activity of the one who believes. Secondly, there is the excellence and worth of the thing believed in. And there are two kinds of righteousness: one resulting from love, and one resulting from fear. For that reason, it is said, "The fear of the Lord is pure, enduring for ever and ever." (Ps. 19:9) Yet, even those who turn to faith and righteousness because of fear (rather than love) will still remain forever. But fear only leads a person to refrain from what is evil. Love, however, leads to the spontaneous doing of good. As a result of love, a person can hear the Lord's words, "I call you no longer servants, but friends." (John 15:15)

Such a person can apply himself confidently to prayer. In his prayers he gives thanks for the past and the present. He also gives thanks for the future, for to him, through faith, the future is already present. He asks to live his present life as one who knows God. He asks for a life free from the flesh. He asks to attain the best things and to flee from the worst. He not only asks *forgiveness* for his sins, but he also asks for help to *repent* and acknowledge his sins.

On his departure, he comes quickly to the One who called him. He is eager to give thanks because of his good conscience. Once he is with Christ, he shows that he is worthy, through his purity, to receive the power of God that is administered through Christ. He receives this power through a process of blending [into Christ]. He does not wish to be warm by merely receiving heat. Neither does he wish to glow by merely reflecting the light of the flame. No, he wants to be light himself.

He properly understands the statement, "Unless you hate father and mother, and your own life, and unless you bear the sign* [you cannot be my disciples]." (Luke 14:26,27) He despises the excessive sentiments of the flesh. For these sentiments contain the powerful spell of pleasure. He has a noble disdain for all things pertaining to the procreation and sustenance of the flesh. He also resists the fleshly element in the soul, putting a bridle bit on the deviant spirit. "For the flesh lusts against the Spirit." (Gal. 5:17) "To bear the sign [of the cross]" is to carry death with you, by saying farewell to the things of the flesh while still alive.

---

i.e., of the cross.

Having made a habit of doing good, he exercises generosity as a natural response—quicker than speaking. He prays that he may help carry the burden of his brothers' sins. For he wants to help his brother to the point of confession and repentance. He is also eager to share his own good things with those dearest to him. Nurturing the seeds planted in him, in accord with the management of the Lord, he continues free of sin. He develops self-control, and he lives in spirit with those who are like him. He is among the choirs of the saints, though he is still detained on earth.

All day and night, he speaks and does the Lord's commands. He rejoices heartily when he wakes up each morning. Not only that, he rejoices at noon, when walking, when in bed, and when dressing and undressing. If he has a son, he teaches him. He is inseparable from the commandments [of God] and from the blessed hope. He is always giving thanks to God, like the living creatures Isaiah mentioned. (Isa. 6:6) He is submissive in every trial, saying "The Lord gave, and the Lord has taken away." (Job 1:21) For Job was that way. After his possessions and health were destroyed, he relinquished everything to the Lord through love. So Job was one who knew God. It is said that Job was "just, holy, and separated from all wickedness." (Job 1:1)

> *The word "holy" sums up all duties toward God and the entire life we are to follow.*

The word "holy" sums up all duties toward God and the entire course of life we are to follow. We must not cling too much to our earthly things, even if they are good. For they are of the body. On the other hand, we shouldn't hate them either, even if they are bad. Rather, we must be above both good and bad. We trample the bad things under foot. And we give the things that are good to those who need them.

12

The Prayer Life Of One Who Knows God

We are commanded to adore and honor the Lord, since we know that he is the Logos*, the Savior, and the Leader. By honoring him, we honor the Father. We are to do this continually in every way throughout our whole lives. It's not something we do just on special days. Of course the elect race [the Jews] were right in saying, "Seven times a day I have praised you." (Ps 119:164) So the one who knows God honors God and thanks him for this knowledge of the way to live. He does this at all times—when alone and when with fellow believers. He doesn't need a special place or a selected temple. He doesn't wait for certain festivals or appointed days. He honors God during his whole life.

A godly man is a good influence on the people around him. He inspires respect and reverence in his associates. Likewise, God influences the person who has uninterrupted fellowship with Him. The one who fellowships with God will grow better in every way: in his conduct, in his speech, and in his character. He is confident that God is always beside him. He doesn't believe that God is confined to certain limited places. So he doesn't think that he can somehow escape God's sight and get away with doing wrong things.

---

*The Greek word *Logos* is generally translated "Word" in our Bibles, but this term also means "Reason." The Logos of God is, of course, Jesus Christ.

We should celebrate God in our entire lives, confident that he is always at our side. So we cultivate our fields, praising God. We sail the sea, singing hymns. In all our conversation we conduct ourselves according to discipline. The one who knows God, then, is closely allied to God. He is always both serious and cheerful. He is serious because his soul is bent toward God. He is cheerful because he constantly thinks of all the blessings that God has given us.

So the one who knows God is truly a kingly man. He is the sacred high priest of God. Even the more advanced of the barbarians recognize the link between priesthood and rulership. For they promote their priestly caste to positions of royal power.

Godly Entertainment

The one who knows God never surrenders himself to the mobs that attend the theaters. Even in his dreams, he is pure from desire of the alluring pleasures that are spoken about, viewed, and practiced. (1 John 2:15-17) He shows no interest in pleasures of sight or in other enjoyments such as expensive incense and perfumes, which bewitch the nostrils. He has no interest in fancy foods or in a great variety of wines, which ensnare the palate. He has no use for elaborate fragrant bouquets, which weaken the soul through the senses. Instead, the one who knows God offers God the first fruits of food, drink and ointments. He makes this offering by recognizing God as the source of all enjoyable things. And he gives thanks for these gifts.

> *We cultivate our fields, praising God.*

The one who knows God rarely goes to banquets or parties, unless he knows that the entertainment will be of a friendly and harmonious nature. For he is convinced that God knows and perceives all things—not just the words, but the thoughts also. In fact, our sense of hearing is not totally a physical thing but one of mental perception. For the mind must interpret different sounds. But God does not have a physical body, needing to hear audible sounds. He does not need senses, as the Stoics mistakenly think. They say that he particularly needs "hearing and sight, for he could never understand any other way."

Unspoken Communication With God

How can anyone say that our voices do not reach God? That they are rolled downward by the air? For the thoughts of the saints can penetrate not only the *air* but the entire *earth*. The divine power sees through the whole soul with the speed of light. So our unspoken desires speak to God, uttering their own kind of voice. Even our own conscience communicates these desires. So what audible voice does God have to wait for? He knows the elect before they are even born. He knows the future as though it had already taken place. Doesn't the light of power shine down to the very bottom of the whole soul? As the Scripture says, "The lamp of knowledge searches the recesses?" (Prov. 20:27) So one could say that God is all ears and all eyes.

In general, an unworthy view of God maintains no holiness—whether in hymns, lectures, writings, or teachings. Instead, it produces ideas and notions that are base and grovelling. Therefore, to receive the praises of the crowds is really to receive condemnation. For the crowds are ignorant of the truth.

Actually, then, our very desires and aspirations—the mind's impulses—are types of prayers. The one who knows God prays for and requests the truly good things for his soul. But he also contributes his own efforts to acquire the practice of goodness. He wants to actually *be* good, rather than merely having good *things*.

For this reason, it is essential that the ones who know God pray. For they know God in truth. They have virtues suitable to God. They know what things are really good and what things to pray for in each individual situation. Of course, we realize it's absurd to pray to those who are not really gods as if they were actually gods. But it is similarly ridiculous to ask

God for things that are not truly good. In effect, you're asking to receive evil things that simply masquerade as good.

Nevertheless, there is such a thing as praying for the prevention of evil. This kind of prayer is never to be used to injure another person. However, the one who knows God, in devotion to righteousness, may use this kind of prayer on behalf of those who are beyond feeling.

To speak more boldly, prayer is conversation with God. Even though we speak in silence, not opening our lips, inwardly we are crying out. And God continually hears all this inward conversation. So also we raise our heads and lift our hands to heaven and set our feet in motion at the closing prayers. As we pray, we try, so to speak, to separate our bodies from the earth. We raise the soul to heaven, winged with yearnings for better things. And so we drive the soul to the region of holiness, casting off the chains of the flesh. For we know quite well that the one who knows God leaves behind the whole world, just as the Jews left Egypt behind. Above all, he wants to be as near as possible to God.

Some people assign specific hours for prayer—such as the third, sixth and ninth hours. But the one who knows God prays throughout his entire life, having [continual] fellowship with God through prayer. When he reaches this fellowship, he leaves behind him all useless things [of this world]. For he has now reached the fullness of one who acts by love. But the division of the day into three prayer times is understood by those who are familiar with the blessed triad of the holy dwellings.

The Heretics Say Prayer Is Unnecessary

At this point, I want to address the teachings of some of the heretics who say that prayer is unnecessary. But the man of God does not listen to heretics.[†] For the only truly holy and righteous man is the who knows God *according to the rule of the church.* Only this man has his verbal and unspoken prayers answered according to the will of God. Since God can do anything he wants, the man who truly knows God receives all that he asks for. For God knows who among all mankind are worthy of good things and who are not. So he gives to each person what is suitable. He does not give to those who do not deserve, even though they ask often. But he does give to those who are worthy. And even though God often gives good things without our asking, this doesn't mean that prayer is unnecessary.

The person who truly knows God gives thanks to God and prays for the conversion of his neighbors. The Lord prayed in this way, giving thanks for the completion of his ministry and praying that as many as possible might be saved. He prayed that people would be saved so that God would be glorified in their salvation. And he prayed that many would acknowledge him who alone is Good and him who alone is Saviour, through the Son, from age to age.

When a person believes he will receive from God, his faith is in itself a type of prayer. It is prayer stored away. Since any occasion to converse with God is prayer, we should miss no opportunity to talk to God.

God is not involuntarily good, in the way that a fire is involuntarily hot. No, it is completely voluntary on God's part to give good things, whether or not he has been asked. No one is saved against his will, for man is not some inanimate object. Rather, we run to salvation voluntarily and of our own free choice. Man received the commandments so that he could choose for himself what things to do and what things to avoid. God does not do good because he has no other choice. Rather, his free choice blesses those who spontaneously turn to him.

The care that God gives us is not like the service that servants give to their masters. Instead, God bestows his care out of compassion for our weakness. So his care is like the care a shepherd gives to his sheep. Or that a king gives to his subjects. And we must be obedient to our appointed leaders who are commissioned by God to direct us.

Therefore, the people who actually render the freest and most kingly service on earth are the servants and attendants of God. They do this because they have knowledge and a righteous mind. So, in reality, every place where we think about God is a sacred place. And every occasion when we think about God is a sacred occasion.

When a man possesses a thankful heart, chooses what is right, and then makes his request in prayer, he himself plays a role in receiving what he asks for. Through prayer, he eagerly grasps the thing he desires. For when the Giver of all good things sees that we are receptive, all good things follow as soon as we think of them. Our character is sifted through prayer, revealing how it stands with respect to duty.

God has given us vocal chords and speech so that we can communicate with each other. But God hears the soul and the mind directly, since soul hears soul and mind hears mind. God doesn't wait for audible voices, as do human interpreters, for he already knows everyone's thoughts. The things that are expressed to us by *voices* are expressed to God by our *thoughts*. Before the beginning of creation, he already knew what our thoughts would be. Therefore we may pray without our voices. We do this by concentrating our whole spiritual natures on expressing our thoughts to God, turning to him with no distractions.

> Our character is sifted through prayer.

Every dawn is a replica of the day of birth. Light begins each morning as only a small point in the midst of darkness. But it gets brighter and brighter as the day goes on. In the same way, the dawn of a new day of knowledge of truth shines forth on those lost in spiritual darkness. As the sun rises in the east, so we pray looking toward the sunrise in the east.* Even the most ancient [pagan] temples used to look toward the west. This was so the people would learn to turn to the east when facing the images. The Psalms say, "Let my prayer be directed before you as incense, the uplifting of my hands as the evening sacrifice." (Ps. 116:2)

---

*It was customary among early Christians to pray facing the east As widespread as this practice was in the second century, this custom probably originated during the days of the apostles. Nevertheless, this was a custom only, and not a commandment that was binding on Christians.

The Prayer Life Of One Who Knows God

However, when evil men pray, their prayers can actually bring harm to them. They can also bring harm to others. If they pray for and receive the things they consider to be good fortune, it will only bring them harm. This is because they are ignorant of how to use these things. For evil men pray to acquire the things they don't have, and they ask for things that *seem* to be good, but really aren't. (Jas. 4:3) The man who knows God simply asks to be able to keep the things he already has. He asks to be able to adapt to whatever the future brings. He seeks eternity for the things he will receive.

The man who knows God prays to receive and to keep the things that are really good—the things that concern the *soul*. This man is content with what he has. He doesn't desire things he doesn't have. For he does not lack any good thing that he really needs. His needs have been supplied through divine grace and knowledge. Since he has everything he needs in himself, he does not want other things. He knows the mind of God and he receives good things as soon as he prays. He is in close contact with the almighty power. He earnestly desires to be spirit-minded. Because of these things, through boundless love, he is united to the Spirit.

13

Holiness: A Joint Project

Being of noble character, the one who knows God gives himself to meditation. And he retains in his soul the permanent energy of the very thing he meditates about. He possesses the most precious thing of all—keen perception [of the divine.] He strives to his utmost to acquire this power by controlling all the [outside] influences that attack his mind. He ponders and meditates without ceasing. He disciplines himself to do without pleasures. He conducts himself righteously in whatever he does.

He can speak wisely and freely, without hiding the things that need to be said at the proper time. He can do this because he has experience, not only in study, but in living the [Christian] life. He has the power of plain speech rather than the power of a babbling tongue. He knows of the things of God from the mystic choir of truth itself. Therefore, he is able to encourage the greatness of righteousness in a way that is worthy. The inspired elevation of his prayer life demonstrates his true righteousness.

He is always mild and meek, accessible, pleasant, long-suffering, and grateful. And he always holds a good conscience. Such a man is strict with himself, not merely to avoid *corruption*, but to avoid *temptation*. For he never puts his soul at risk of being conquered by either pleasure or pain. When the Logos (who is the Judge) calls, he is ready. Being spiritually uncompromising, not indulging the flesh at all, he is able to walk unswervingly where justice directs him to go. He is able to do this because he is persuaded that all things are being well-managed [by God].

He believes that all souls who have chosen righteousness will progress in their growth until they come to the ultimate Good itself—to the entryway of the Father's house, close to the great High Priest. This is the one who knows God: the one who is sure that the affairs of the universe are managed in the best possible way. He is pleased with everything that happens. It stands to reason, then, that he would not plead with God for the necessities of life. He knows that God, who knows everything, gives the righteous everything they need even though they do not ask.

In my opinion, God supplies all things to a man of art according to the rules of art. And to the [unbelieving] Gentile, he supplies in a way that befits a Gentile. Likewise, he bestows to the one who knows God in a way that befits such a person. For example, a man who merely leaves the Gentiles will ask for *faith*. But a person who ascends to the heights of knowing God will ask for the perfection of *love*. And the one who knows God, who has reached the summit, prays differently than the common man. The common man prays for continual good *health*. But the one who knows God prays that his *contemplation* [of God] will grow and abide.

The one who knows God will pray that he will never fall from righteousness. And he gives his most strenuous cooperation in order to never fall. For he knows that some of the angels were hurled to the earth through their own carelessness. Those angels had not yet reached that state of oneness. They never freed themselves from the natural inclination towards being double-minded.

All things relating to time and place help him who has trained himself to the summit of knowledge and has raised himself to the height of the perfect man. He has made it his choice to live without transgressing. He disciplines himself in order to attain the stability of knowledge on all sides. Yet, if part of him is still weighed down by the flesh, it will drag down the part of him that had been elevated by faith.

Therefore, the person who knows God acquires a moral excellence that cannot be lost. So [good] habits become part of his nature. And just as a stone can never lose its weight, so such a person can never lose his knowledge. His moral excellence reaches this point (of never being able to be lost) through four things: (1) knowledge, (2) the exercise of his will, (3) the force of reason, and (4) the power of God. It is only through this care that moral excellence becomes incapable of being lost. So the one who knows God will be cautious in order to avoid sinning. He will use his faculties to avoid losing this righteousness.

Knowledge produces contemplation by teaching a person to recognize the things that contribute to the permanence of righteousness. The highest thing is the knowledge of God. (John 17:3) This knowledge preserves righteousness in such a way as to make it incapable of being lost. And he who knows God is holy and righteous. In fact, the only righteous person is the one who knows God.

The one who knows God rejoices in good things that are *present*. And he is joyful about those things that are *promised*. For he views them as though they were already present. So the promised things don't escape his notice, as though they were still absent. He foreknows what kinds of things they are. Because of his knowledge [of God], he knows what each future thing will be like. So, in a sense, he already possesses those things. As far as possible, our man who knows God possesses all godly qualities. But he doesn't necessarily possess them to the same degree as someone else might. Otherwise, there would be no room for advancement.

> God gives closer supervision to those who know him, and he thereby honors them.

How God Empowers Those Who Know Him

God gives closer supervision to those who know him, and in this way he honors them. After all, weren't all things made for the sake of good men? Aren't all things for them to possess and enjoy, or rather to assist in their salvation? Therefore, God will not deprive such persons (for whom all things were created) of the things that exist for the sake of righteousness. God infuses those who have chosen the good life with strength for the rest of their salvation. He evidently does this in honor of their holy choice and their excellent nature.

The one who knows God can have every kind of goodness produced in him, just as long as it is his goal to know and do everything with understanding. A physician can help a person become and remain healthy only if that person cooperates with the physician in his recuperation. Likewise, God gives eternal salvation to those who work jointly with him in the attainment of knowledge and right conduct. We have the power to avoid the things the commandments forbid. And we also have the power to obey God's commandments.

I can think of a good illustration from Greek history. After working and training hard for a long time, a famous athlete was journeying to the Olympic games. On the way, he passed a statue of Zeus and looked up at it. "O Zeus," he prayed, "if I have prepared perfectly for this contest, then please give me the victory, as it is only fair." It is the same for the one who knows God. If he has blamelessly and with good conscience done all that he can do, all things will work to carry his salvation on to completion. In other words, God expects *us* to do the things that are in our own power to do. He will do the rest.[†]

Therefore, a person who wants to converse with God must have his soul immaculate and pure, without stain. It is essential for him to make himself perfectly good. But it is best for this person to make his prayers gently with those who are good. For it is dangerous to take part in the sins of others.

Therefore, the one who knows God will pray with a person who has recently become a believer about the things that the two of them have a duty to act on together. Actually, his whole life is a holy festival! His sacrifices consist of many things: Prayers, praise, and Scripture readings before meals. Psalms and hymns during meals and before bed. And prayers again during the night. By these sacrifices, he joins himself to the divine choir. For he continually ponders over these things.

And what? Doesn't the one who knows God offer the other kind of sacrifice as well? I mean the one that consists of giving instruction and money to those who need? Of course he does! But he doesn't spout forth long, wordy prayers with his mouth. Rather, he has learned to simply ask the Lord for the things that are necessary. (Matt. 6:11) He prays everywhere, but not in a showy way for everyone to see. (Matt. 6:5,6) He prays at every opportunity—while walking, while talking, while silent, while reading or while working.

He can communicate with God simply by forming a thought in the most secret part of his soul—calling on the Father "with unspoken groanings." For the Father is at his side, even while he is still speaking. Since there are only three goals of any action, the one who knows God concentrates on the goals of excellence and usefulness. He does nothing toward the goal of pleasure, leaving that for people who pursue the common life.

14

To Know God Is To Become Like Him

To know God is to be molded after his image and likeness. The one who knows God imitates God in every way possible. He is missing none of the things that contribute to his being like God. He practices self-control and endurance. He lives righteously and rules his own emotions. To the extent possible, he gives what he has to others, and he does good in both word and deed. For it is written, "He is the greatest in the kingdom who is both a doer and a teacher." (Matt. 5:19) Such a person imitates God by blessing others. For God's gifts are for the common good.

It is said, "Whoever attempts to do anything with presumption, provokes God." (Num. 15:30) Haughtiness is a defect of the soul. We should repent of it the same as we repent of other sins.

There are three parts of our body that we need to adjust in order to grow spiritually: the mouth (speech), the heart (the power to will), and the hands (action). It has been beautifully spoken of those who repent: "This day you have chosen God to be your God; and this day God has chosen you to be his people." (Deut. 26:17,18) God—the Self-Existent One—adopts the person who pleads with him and who is quick to serve him. Even though such a person is only one in number, he is honored equally with the rest of the church. For since he is a part of the church, he makes the body of Christ complete.

Nobility Is Not Something You're Born Into

True nobility is demonstrated by choosing and practicing that which is best. The status of one's birth makes no difference.† After all, how did it benefit Adam to have his noble origin? His father was no mere human! Rather, he himself was the father of all men. Yet, he readily chose that which was dishonorable, following the lead of his wife. He neglected that which was true and good. As a result, he traded his immortal life for a mortal one—but not forever.

In contrast, Noah—whose origin was not as lofty as Adam's—was saved by divine care. For he dedicated himself to God. Look also at Abraham. He had children by three different wives. (I don't think he did this for the indulgence of pleasure, but for the purpose of multiplying mankind during that early period of the human race.) Nevertheless, despite his many children, he was succeeded by only one, who was the heir of Abraham's blessings. The rest were separated from the family.

Similarly, Abraham's son [Isaac] fathered twins. Of these twins, the younger won his father's blessing and received his prayers. So he became the heir, and his older brother served him. This was actually to the older brother's benefit. For the greatest blessing one can give an unrighteous man is to prevent him from being his own master.

All these things had symbolic and prophetic significance. Scripture clearly indicates that all things belong to the wise, saying, "Because God has had mercy on me, I have all things." (Gen. 33:11) So Scripture teaches that we are to desire only one thing [divine wisdom]. All other things stem from this. And the worthy receive what has been promised. Accordingly, through divine wisdom, a righteous man becomes an heir of the kingdom. Scripture thereby views him as being a fellow citizen with the righteous ones of old. The deeds of those ancient ones—who lived according to law both before and after the Law was given—have become examples to us.

Scripture teaches that the wise man is, in effect, a king. For example, it mentions that foreigners said to Abraham, "You are a king among us before God." (Gen. 23:6) Those foreigners obeyed the good man [Abraham] of their own accord because they admired his moral excellence. Even Plato the philosopher taught that the goal of happiness is to become molded into the image of God, to the extent possible.

15

You Cannot Know God Without Faith

A person is not born with faith.† The apostle says that faith comes through hearing. And we hear through the word of God. "How will they call on him in whom they have not believed? And how will they believe on him of whom they have not heard? And how will they hear without a preacher? And how will they preach unless they are sent? As it is written, 'How beautiful are the feet of those who publish glad tidings of good things!'" (Rom. 10:14,15) Notice how Paul ties faith and hearing together. He shows that the preaching of the apostles leads to faith in the Son of God.

The Benefits Of Faith

One benefit of faith is that it enables us to learn from God.† The game of ball illustrates how this works. Playing ball depends on two things: The first player must throw the ball with skill. And the second player must catch it with dexterity. Similarly, teaching is best accomplished when those hearing have faith. The very best instruction is useless without a receptive student. Even prophecy is of no avail without a believing listener.

This same principle is seen in God's creation.† Seeds can't grow without the productive power of the earth. A fire is not easily started without a bundle of dry twigs. Just like a magnet attracts steel, faith attracts instruction.

Another benefit of faith is that it brings about repentance. Unless a man believes that the thing to which he is addicted is sin, he will not abandon it. He will not reform unless he believes that punishment is imminent for sinners, and that those living by the commandments will receive salvation.

The divine Logos cries out, calling all mankind together. He knows perfectly well who will not obey. Still, to obey or disobey is in our own power, provided we are not ignorant of the options. God justly demands from each of us according to our ability. Some are not yet *able* to obey, but they are at least *willing*. Others, through practice and purification, are both willing *and* able to obey. The soul has power to will, but it cannot act without the body.

Furthermore, God does not evaluate actions by their results alone. Rather, he also looks at the degree of free choice in the action. For example, one person might help his neighbor because he wants to.† Another may do it only because he was forced to.†

There is a difference between repentance and innocence.† Repentance comes when a person recognizes a transgression *after* he commits it. But innocence means that a person has knowledge of right and wrong *beforehand* [and so he doesn't transgress].

Another benefit of faith is that it leads to hope.† For hope is based on faith. A person has hope when he actually *expects* to possess the good things promised. This expectation comes from faith.

What It Means To Be Faithful

A person who is faithful safeguards the things that have been entrusted to him. He doesn't betray the trust. We Christians have been entrusted with the divine utterances and the divine commands. We also have the obligation to *obey* them. The one keeping this trust is the faithful servant who will be praised by the Lord.

When it is said, "God is faithful," it means that he can be believed no matter what he says. We believe God and can place our confidence in him regarding our salvation. We confide in him because we know he will not fail to do the things he has promised to us nor fail to give us the things he created for us. To have charitable generosity is to want someone else to have good things. God needs nothing, so his generosity and goodness are directed to *us* for our benefit.

The Gentiles Are Saved By Faith

Abraham's faith was considered righteousness. Since we are his descendants, we must also believe through hearing. We are Israelites, being convinced by hearing—not by signs. The prophets said, "Rejoice, childless ones; break forth and cry, you who did not go through the pain of childbirth. For the children of the desolate will number more than those of the woman with a husband." (Isa. 54:1) It was also said, "You have lived for the fence of the people, your children were blessed in their fathers' tents." Since the same mansions promised by prophecy to the patriarchs are also promised to us, we see that the God of both covenants is the same.* And therefore the words were added, "You have inherited the covenant of Israel." This clearly refers to those nations that were once considered to be barren because they did not have God's Word.

The apostle says in his letter to the Romans, "For the righteousness of God is revealed from faith to faith." (Rom. 1:17) So he taught about the one salvation that is perfected from the prophets to the Gospel by one Lord. He says, "I commit this task to you, my son Timothy, so that in agreement with the prophecies before you, you might fight a good battle; holding both faith and a good conscience. Some who have put away these things have made shipwreck of their faith," because, through unbelief, they have stained the conscience God gave them. (1 Tim. 1:18,19)

---

*The Gnostics taught that the God of the Old Testament was a different Being than the God of the New Testament.

So faith cannot be belittled as simple and common. If it were a mere human trait, as the Greeks assumed, it would have passed away. But because it grows and flourishes everywhere, I assert that faith is something divine. It cannot be torn apart by friendship nor dissolved by the presence of fear. Love makes men believers because of its connection with faith. Faith, the foundation of love, introduces the doing of good. Faith is truly the first step toward salvation. Faith, fear, hope, repentance, self-control, and patience—these things lead us to love and knowledge.

The Apostle Barnabas says, "From what I have received, I have been diligent to send bit by bit to you; that with your faith you may also have perfect knowledge. Fear and patience are helpers of your faith; and our allies are patience and self-control. Continuing in purity, these are accompanied by wisdom, understanding, intelligence, and knowledge."* These virtues are the things making up knowledge. So actually faith is more fundamental than any of these virtues. It's as necessary to life as breathing is. Just as it's impossible to live without air, so it's impossible to acquire knowledge without faith. In short, faith is the foundation of truth.

> *Faith is as necessary to life as breathing is.*

---

*From the *Letter of Barnabas*. Many early churches believed this letter was written by the companion of the Apostle Paul, and they therefore included it in their New Testament canon.

16

To Know God Is To Love Others

Clement [of Rome] says, "Our love for mankind seeks the common good."* But to seek the common good sometimes means we must suffer as a martyr. Other times, it requires us to teach by both word and deed. This is love—to love God and to love our neighbor. Clement continues, "This [love] carries us to indescribable heights. Furthermore, 'love covers a multitude of sins.' 'Love bears all things and suffers all things.' Love joins us to God and enables us to do everything harmoniously. The chosen ones of God were perfected in love. Apart from love, nothing is well pleasing to God. Who is fit to be found in it, except those whom God counts worthy?"* The Apostle Paul says, "If I give my body, and have not love, I am a sounding [piece of] brass and a tinkling cymbal." (1 Cor. 13:1,3)

If I simply confess the Lord out of fear, or in expectation of reward, I am an ordinary man. I may use the Lord's name, but I do not really *know* him. For there are people who love only with their lips. There are even those who give their bodies to be burned. But Paul says, "If I give all my goods to the poor" but not out of love, "I am nothing." For I have given

---

*From the *Letter to the Corinthians* written by Clement of Rome around 95 A.D. Many early churches included this letter in their New Testament canon. Clement of *Rome* should not be confused with Clement of *Alexandria*.

with thought of reward—either from the one I have helped, or from the Lord. Paul further says, "If I have all faith so as to remove mountains," but I am not faithful to the Lord because of love, "I am nothing." (1 Cor. 13:3)

Love Hates Sin

Love does not permit sin. Yet, if a man with love falls into any sin because of the interference of the adversary, he will imitate David. Like David he will sing, "I will confess unto the Lord, and it will please him more than a young bull that has horns and hoofs. Let the poor see it and be glad." For he says, "Sacrifice to God a sacrifice of praise, and pay your vows to the Lord. Call upon me in the day of trouble, and I will deliver you, and you shall glorify me." (Ps. 50:13-15) "For the sacrifice of God is a broken spirit." (Ps. 51:17)

As it is said, "God is love." (1 Jn. 4:8) And he is good. Love "works no injury to one's neighbor." (Rom. 13:10) It never injures or extracts revenge. In short, it does good to all according to the image of God. So "love is the fulfillment of the Law." (Rom. 13:10) For example, love fulfills the commands to not commit adultery and to not covet your neighbor's wife. In the past, those sins were prohibited through fear. But now we obey them out of love.[†]

All the generations from Adam to the present day are gone. But those who have been perfected in love, through the grace of God, hold the place of the godly. And the godly shall be manifested when the kingdom of Christ comes.

Even though two deeds may be identical, they can differ in quality, depending on the motive behind them. For it makes a difference whether a deed is done out of fear or out of love. Appropriately, then, the reward is different, depending on the motive. The reward that awaits the one who knows God is that which "eye has not seen, ear has not heard, and mind has not conceived." (1 Cor. 2:9) But the reward awaiting the one who has merely exercised elementary faith is the promise to receive a hundredfold that which he has left. (Matt. 19:29) It's still a magnificent reward.[†] But it's a reward that humans can comprehend. In contrast, the reward that awaits the one who knows God is beyond human comprehension.

Love Does Not Lust

I remember a certain man who considered himself to be one who knew God. Once he expounded on the words, "But I say unto you, he that looks on a woman to lust after, has committed adultery." (Matt. 5:28) His explanation of this passage was that Jesus was not condemning the bare desire [for a woman]. Rather, as he explained, what Jesus condemned was actually imagining having sex with another woman.

His explanation reminds me of the judicial decision of Bocchoris the Just, which historians have written about: A certain young man felt passionate love for a prostitute. So he persuaded her to come to him the next day. And he agreed he would pay her a stipulated amount for doing so. However, that night he dreamed of having sex with her. And the dream satisfied his desire. So when the prostitute came to him the next day as agreed, he turned her away.

Later, however, she learned of what had taken place in his dream. And she demanded payment from him. But he refused.[†] So they both went before the judge. Hearing the story, the judge ordered the young man to take out his purse and hold it out in the sunlight. He then told the prostitute that she could grab the shadow as payment. In other words, he facetiously ordered the young man to give the *image* of payment in exchange for the *image* of an embrace.

> **Chaste love does not admire the beauty of the flesh. It admires the beauty of the spirit.**

But Jesus condemns more than just imagining having sex with a woman. For to fantasize is to already commit an act of lust. Rather, Jesus goes further.[†] He condemns any man who looks on the beauty of a woman with carnal and sinful admiration. It is a different matter, however, to look on beauty with chaste love. Chaste love does not admire the beauty of the flesh. It admires the beauty of the spirit. With such love, a person sees the body only as an image. His admiration carries him to the Artist himself—to true beauty.

17

How To Be Made Into The Image Of God

The one who knows God has a true and grand view of the universe because he is receptive to divine instruction. When he first heard about God and his loving guidance, he readily believed because he already stood in awe of Creation. Then, once he demonstrated his ability to learn, he became an eager pupil of the Lord. Now he devotes all his energy to learning, doing everything to obtain the knowledge he desires. He understands that the Lord is the one "who teaches man knowledge," as the prophet has said. (Mic. 4:2)

As faith progresses, his desire for investigation increases. In this way the one who knows God tastes the very will of God. He yields his *soul*, not just his ears, to the things spoken. Because he understands the essence and principles of the things spoken, he conforms his soul to what is essential. The one who knows God understands biblical commands in a different way than most people. I'm speaking of commands such as, "Do not commit adultery" and "Do not kill." Others see only the commands, but the one who knows God understands the spirit of the law.†

In accord with what is right, he never prefers the pleasant to the beneficial. This would be true even if he found himself in circumstances where a beautiful woman tried to entice him and wantonly urged him on. For example, Joseph remained steadfast when his master's wife tried to seduce him. As she forcibly held his coat, he left it with her, becoming bare of sin, but clothed with good character. Even though Joseph's Egyptian master could not see what he was doing, the Almighty did. We humans merely hear what people say, and we see their outward appearance. But God examines the source of the words and appearance.

Though sickness, misfortune, and even death come upon the one who knows God, he remains unyielding in his soul. He knows that these things are a part of earthly life. He also knows that by God's power, they become the instruments of salvation. They bring necessary discipline to those who are difficult to reform. By God's guidance, troubles are distributed according to need.

The one who knows God also enjoys God's creatures. Out of thankfulness to the Creator, he uses them as the Logos determines, and only to the extent he determines.

He never cherishes resentment, and he never harbors a grudge against anyone. This is true even though somebody deserves to be hated for his conduct. But because he worships the Maker, the one who knows God loves such hateful persons. He realizes that even those people are fellow sharers in the gift of [earthly] life. He feels compassion for them because of their ignorance, and he prays for them.

Of course, the one who knows God is still subject to the weaknesses and ailments of the body. In situations he cannot control, he withdraws himself from troubles and goes to the things which really belong to him. So he is not carried away by what is foreign to him. He only finds room for those things which are necessary, so his soul is preserved unharmed. For he does not wish to only appear to be faithful. He wants to truly be faithful in word and deed. He not only praises what is noble, but strives to be noble himself. Because of love, he changes from a good and faithful servant into a friend. He continues to perfect the habits he obtained from true instruction and great discipline.

> By God's guidance, troubles are distributed according to need.

The one who knows God strives to attain the height of knowledge. His character is sterling. He is composed in his conduct. He possesses all the advantages that belong to the one who knows God. His role models are the many patriarchs who lived righteously—and the innumerable prophets and angels. But his greatest model is the Lord himself, who not only taught, but demonstrated, that it is possible for humans to attain that highest life of all. So the one who knows God does not love the good things of the world, even though they are within his grasp. For he does not want to remain on the earth, but desires to attain the things hoped for. (1 John 2:15-17)

> *He should consider his marriage inseparable from his love of the Lord.*

He endures toils, trials, and afflictions. But his endurance is not like that of the philosophers. They courageously endured suffering in the hope that their present troubles would eventually end. But the one who knows God endures suffering with the conviction that he will receive his *future* hopes. So he is above not only the *pains* of this world but its *pleasures* as well.

They say that Peter, on seeing his wife led to death, rejoiced because she was being taken home. He called to her with encouragement and comfort. Addressing her by name, he shouted, "Remember the Lord!" Such was the marriage of the blessed. Such was their perfect disposition toward those dearest to them.

So the apostle says, "He who marries should be as though he was unmarried." (1 Cor. 7:29) He should consider his marriage inseparable from his love of the Lord. His affection for his wife should be subordinate to that of the Lord. That is why Peter could encourage his wife to look forward to her departure from this life to the Lord.

The faithful who suffered for God obviously believed in blessings after death, didn't they? For they gave thanks to

God even during the worst part of their punishments? Their faith was firm, and it was followed by works of faith.

The one who knows God is also prudent in human affairs, judging what should be done by the just man. He received his principles from God, and he patterns himself after the divine image. So he is moderate in both pains and pleasures of the body. He boldly struggles against his fears, trusting in God. His soul is beautified with perfect moral excellence. It is the earthly image of the divine Power. His soul has developed through the joint actions of nature, training, and reason.

When the soul has conformed to the gospel in every facet of life, it becomes a temple of the Holy Spirit. Such a person withstands every type of fear—no matter how terrible. He endures poverty, disease, public disgrace, and even death. He is unconquered by pleasure, and he is lord over his own fleshly desires. He knows very well which things should be done and which should not. He also knows what to fear, and what not to fear. So he understands what the Logos indicates is necessary. He distinguishes what truly *is* good from what only *appears* to be good. And he distinguishes those things that really should be feared from those things most humans commonly fear—such as death, disease, and poverty.

The truly good man is without fleshly desires. He has transcended the whole life of fleshly desires because his soul is now endowed with moral excellence. The good man does not fear those occurrences that are considered terrible by other men, for they are not truly evil. The evil things that should be dreaded are no part of the one who knows God, since they have no part with the good. It is impossible for contrary things to meet in the same person at the same time. The one who flawlessly acts out the drama of life, which God has given him to play, knows both what is to be accomplished and what is to be endured.

On Martyrdom

Doesn't cowardice arise from ignorance of what should and should not be feared? So the only truly courageous man is the one who knows God. For he knows both present and future good things. And, as I have said, he also knows which things should not be feared. He knows that evil should be hated. He realizes that it destroys that which brings true knowledge. Therefore, protected by God's armor, he makes war against evil.

No one who is irrationally brave is a person who knows God. One might call children brave, but they do dangerou things because of ignorance. For example, they often touch fire itself. Likewise, wild beasts that rush up to the points of spears have a brute courage that might be called valiant. Some people might call acrobats valiant, because they skillfully somersault on swords, performing their tricks for mere monetary gain.

But the truly brave man, seeing the danger from the mob surrounding him, courageously awaits whatever comes. Some who are called martyrs bring perils upon themselves and purposefully rush into the heart of danger. But the truly brave man sensibly protects himself until God calls him. Then he promptly surrenders himself and confirms the call, not wanting to be impulsive. He then offers himself to be proved in the exercise of true, rational courage. He does not endure small dangers in order to avoid greater ones. He does not fear criticism from his equals or those of like feelings. But he continues in the confession of his calling. He willingly obeys the call out of love for God—not for the sake of reward. He has no other purpose than pleasing God.

Some people suffer because they want [human] glory. Others suffer because they fear some worse punishment [from God]. Still others suffer because of their hope of receiving pleasures and delights after death, being *children* in faith. All of these are blessed, but none of them have yet become mature in the faith. They have not come to know God in the fullest sense. In gymnastic contests, there are crowns for men, and then there are crowns for children. It's the same in the church. Love should be chosen for itself, and for nothing else. So, along with his knowledge, the one who knows God develops the perfection of fortitude. For he has studied to gain mastery over the flesh.

Being Spiritually Fit

In all circumstances, the soul of the one who knows God is strong. It's healthy and robust, like the body of an athlete. Love makes the spiritual athlete fearless and brave. He is confident in the Lord, for love anoints and trains him. Righteousness assures truthfulness in his whole life. "Let your yes be yes; and your no, no"—that is the epitome of righteousness.

The same is true of self-control. It should not be practiced for love of honor, the way athletes do for the sake of crowns and fame. Neither should it be practiced for love of money. Some pretend to exercise self-control, but they pursue what is good only with terrible suffering. Nor does the Christian practice self-control simply for the healthful benefits to the body.

Furthermore, an uncultured man who has never tasted pleasures is not necessarily practicing self-control. Many who have led such lives lose all self-control when they finally taste pleasures for the first time. These are the ones who are only restrained by law and fear. But upon finding a favorable opportunity, they abandon good. But true self-control, desirable for its own sake, is perfected through knowledge. It is ever enduring, making the man the lord and master of himself. So the one who knows God is moderate and free from fleshly desires. He is incapable of being dissolved by pleasures and pains.

The source of these virtues is love. (Col. 3:14) It is the most sacred and sovereign knowledge of all. By serving what is best and most exalted, love renders the one who knows God into both a friend and a son [of God]. In the soil of truth, love has grown "a perfect man, up to the measure of full stature." (Eph. 4:13)

When two things are in agreement, they become one. The one who knows God, because he loves the one true God, is the only man who is really complete. He is a friend of God and is even made a son. This then is the crowning step for the soul of the one who knows God. He receives this crowning step only when he has become quite pure and is considered worthy to eternally behold God Almighty "face to face," so to speak. Having become totally spirit-natured, having become of kindred nature to the spirit-natured church, the soul of the one who knows God abides in God's rest. (Heb. 4:9-11)

18

Oaths And Lawsuits

The man who has a proven character and is devoted to God is not at all given to lying and swearing. An oath is a very serious affirmation, and it involves taking the Lord's name. So how can such a man, who has been proven faithful, show himself to be unfaithful so as to need an oath? Isn't his very life a sure and decisive oath? By the sure, unwavering way he lives and speaks, he shows that he is truthful. Therefore, the one who knows God will never lie or perjure himself. For to do so would be to wrong God. We can't actually *harm* God, but we can *wrong* him.

Another reason he will avoid lying or wrongdoing is so he won't harm his neighbor. For he has learned to love his neighbor. And his "neighbor" includes people who are not his intimate friends. Finally, for his own sake, he avoids lying or breaking an oath. For he surely does not want to wrong himself.

Actually, the one who knows God does not even swear. He prefers to affirm by saying "yes" and to deny by saying "no." For it is an oath to swear, or to promise in any way resembling an oath. If another person needs to perceive the certainty of his answer, the Christian can simply add to his affirmation or denial the words, "I speak truthfully." At the same time, his life should be lived in such a way that outsiders have complete confidence in him. The result is that unbelievers will feel no need to ask the man of God to take an oath. His life should also inspire good feeling in himself and the people around him. This is voluntary righteousness.

The one who knows God swears truly, but he is not inclined to swear at all. He rarely comes near to an oath, as we have already said. His speaking truth on oath is a result of his agreement with the truth. Speaking the truth on oath is simply a result of correctness in duties. So why would it be necessary for this man to take an oath, since he lives a life in accord with the pinnacle of truth? He, then, who does not even swear will be far from perjuring himself. And he who does not breach his agreements, will never swear. For an agreement is violated or upheld by actions. Lying and perjury in affirming and swearing are wrong. But the one who knows God should live a just life, and he should never fail in his duties. As a result, his actions swear to the truth for him. Therefore, it is unnecessary for him to swear with his mouth.

The one who knows God is satisfied only with God's consciousness and with his own consciousness. He knows that God is everywhere. He is not afraid to tell the truth, and he knows it is unworthy of him to lie. So he does not lie, and he never does anything contrary to his agreements. And so he does not swear, even when he is asked for his oath. And he never denies what is true, even if he is tortured to death.*

Lawsuits

I have said that the one who knows God is free from fleshly desires. By 'advancing in love,' the perfection of the believer "comes to a perfect man—to the measure of full stature." (Eph. 4:13) He is assimilated to God and becomes truly angelic. I could continue with many other testimonies from the Scriptures to support this view. But my discourse has become rather long. So it would be better for those who desire to study it more to build on what has been said by selecting additional passages from the Scriptures.

---

*A Christian could escape torture and death simply by lying and saying he was not a Christian.

Nevertheless, I will mention one passage [of Scripture] so as to not leave this whole matter without scriptural proof. In the first letter to the Corinthians, the divine apostle says, "If any of you have a dispute against another, do you dare to go to law before the unrighteous, and not before the saints? Don't you know that the saints shall judge the world?" (1 Cor. 6:2)

This section of Scripture from which I have quoted is rather long. So we will simply look at the most pertinent passages to demonstrate the meaning of the apostle's words. And I will only briefly explain this discourse in which the apostle describes the perfection of the one who knows God. For he does not characterize this one as someone who merely *suffers* wrong rather than *doing* wrong. Rather, he teaches that the one who knows God does not even *remember* wrongs. In fact, the apostle does not even allow this one to pray against the person who has done wrong to him. The one who knows God realizes that the Lord specifically said that we should 'pray *for* our enemies.' (Matt. 5:44)

If someone who has been wronged goes to court before the unrighteous, he obviously wishes to retaliate. He shows a desire to injure the other person in return. This means he is also doing wrong himself. The apostle also says that he wishes "some to go to court before the saints." (1 Cor. 6:7,8) This refers to those who pray that the wrongdoer will suffer punishment for their injustice. He implies that these people are better than those who take the sinners to court. But they are not yet obedient. For they have not become entirely free of resentment. And they are not praying *for* their enemies.

It is good, then, for them to receive the right attitudes through repentance. And such repentance results in faith. Even if the truth seems to attract enemies, it itself is not hostile to any one. "God makes his sun to shine on the just and on the unjust." (Matt. 5:45) And he sent the Lord himself to the just and the unjust. He that strives to be like God must be free of resentment. He forgives seventy times seven times throughout his entire life. His entire earthly course is indicated by the enumeration of sevens. So throughout his life he pardons anyone who has done wrong to him.

He realizes that the good man should be willing to turn his property over to those who wrong him. Not only that, he knows that the righteous man should ask the judges to pardon the offenses of those who have wronged him. The reason for this is that external things never really belong to the one who knows God. This includes all things that concern only the physical body—even death of the body.

How can a person judge the apostate angels if he himself has become an apostate by not forgiving injuries as the gospel teaches? For the apostle says, "Why do you not rather suffer wrong? Why are you not rather cheated? Yes, you do wrong and cheat" by praying against those who sin in ignorance. (1 Cor. 6:7,8) You seek to deprive them of the compassion and goodness of God. The apostle refers to the ones who do you injury as "your brothers." By this term, he is referring both to those in the faith and those who may later be in the faith. For someone who is presently hostile to the faith might eventually become a believer. So the logical conclusion is that we should regard *everyone* as a potential brother even if he is not presently in the faith.

> *We should regard everyone as a potential brother even though he is not presently in the faith.*

The one who knows God recognizes all men to be the work of one God. He knows they are all in God's image, even though his image may be seen more clearly in some than in others. He recognizes the work of God in every created person, and again he praises the will of God.

19

Christian Perfection

"Don't you know that the unrighteous shall not inherit the kingdom of God?"(1 Cor. 6:9) And he who retaliates acts unrighteously. It makes no difference if it is by action, word, or desire. For the gospel addresses even the unspoken desire. "And this is what some of you were." And those you don't forgive still are such.

"But you are washed."(1 Cor. 6:11) Not just like everyone else, but with knowledge. You have discarded the fleshly desires of the soul to become, as far as is possible, part of the goodness of God's care. You do this by being long-suffering, and by forgiving both the just and the unjust." (Matt. 5:45) You become like the sun, shining beams of kindliness on others through your words and deeds.

"But you are sanctified."(1 Cor. 6:11) He who has been sanctified is in a condition to be holy. He does not give in to fleshly desires in any way. He behaves as though he were already freed from this body. It is as though he had already grown holy, rising above this earth.

The apostle continues, "For this reason, you are justified in the name of the Lord." (1 Cor. 6:11) God made you to be righteous, just as he is righteous. You are blended as far as possible with the Holy Spirit. "Are not all things lawful to me? Yet I will not be brought under the power of any." (1 Cor. 6:12) For you are not to do, think, or speak anything contrary to the Gospel.

"Meats for the belly, and the belly for meats, which God shall destroy." (1 Cor. 6:13) Some people think and live as though they were made for eating. They don't eat simply for the purpose of sustaining life. To obtain knowledge is not their primary goal. Does God not say that these are in a figurative sense the fleshly parts of the holy body? For the church of the Lord, the spiritual and holy choir, is referred to as a body. So those who are merely called Christians, but do not live in accordance with the Word, are the fleshly parts.

Now, this spiritual body, the holy Church, "is not for fornication." Likewise, we are not to apostatize from the gospel by adopting those things that belong to pagan life. And the one who acts like a pagan in the church, whether in actions, words, or thoughts, commits fornication both as to the church and as to his own body. If his conduct is contrary to the covenant, he "is joined to the harlot." (1 Cor. 6:15) He thereby becomes another "body"—one that is not holy. He becomes "one flesh" with something else, living a pagan life and having a different hope. "But he who is joined to the Lord in spirit" becomes a spiritual body by a different kind of union.

> God made you to be righteous, just as he is righteous.

The one joined to the Lord is fully a son. He is a holy man—one who knows God. He is formed by the teaching of the Lord and is perfect, without fleshly desires. In deed, in word, and in spirit itself, he is being brought close to the Lord. Because he has reached spiritual manhood in this manner, he will receive the mansion that is due to him.

Those who partake of this knowledge will understand how it was said by the Lord, "Be perfect as your Father, perfectly." (Matt. 5:48) We call physicians and philosophers "perfect," don't we? So, likewise, we can call one who knows God "perfect." We become perfect by forgiving sins, forgetting injuries, and living free of fleshly desires every day. However, although all of these things are important, none of them put us on the same plane as God. The Stoics irreverently say that virtue in man and God is the same. But we don't say this. Should we not be perfect, as the Father *wills?* For it is utterly impossible for any one to become perfect as God *is.* The Father wishes us to be perfect by living blamelessly, being obedient to the Gospel.

20

Women Who Know God

It is possible for man and woman to share equally in this perfection of which I'm speaking. For example, Judith became perfect among women. When her city was under siege, she went into the enemy camp, at the entreaty of the elders. She scorned all danger for her country's sake. She gave herself into the enemy's hand in faith in God. And she soon obtained the reward of her faith. Though she was a woman, she prevailed over the enemy of her religion. And she was able to take the head of Holofernes.[1]

Esther is another example of one who was made perfect by faith. She rescued Israel from the power of the king and the cruelty of the satrap. Although she was a lone woman, weak from fasting, she held back ten thousand armed hands. By her faith, she had the tyrant's decree annulled. She appeased the king and restrained Haman. By her perfect prayer to God, she preserved Israel unscathed.

Look also at Susanna and [Miriam], the sister of Moses. [Miriam] was the prophet's companion in commanding the multitude. She was superior to all the women among the Hebrews who were renowned for their wisdom. As for Susanna, in her surpassing modesty she remained the unwavering martyr of chastity. She went to death, condemned by wanton admirers.[2]

---

[1] From the Book of Judith, one of the works included in the *Septuagint*, which was the Old Testament of the early church. The Book of Judith was included in the original King James Version.

[2] The account of Susanna appears at the beginning of the Book of Daniel in the *Septuagint*.

Women Of Wisdom

The wise woman will first choose to persuade her husband to join her in what leads to [true] happiness. But if he does not join her, let her earnestly pursue moral excellence by herself. Yet, she should gain her husband's consent in everything, so as never to do anything against his will. The only exception would be those things that lead to righteousness and salvation. And a man should not keep either his wife or a maid servant from such a way of life. For to do so would be to drive her away from righteousness and sober-mindedness. In effect, he would be choosing to make his own house wicked and morally unrestrained.

In order to be familiar with anything, a man or woman must first be taught, trained, and then given the opportunity to put the things learned into practice. And, as I have said, moral excellence depends on ourselves above all—not on others. Nobody else can suppress those things that depend on ourselves—no matter how hard they try. For the gift is one conferred by God. It is not in the power of any other. So it should be understood that the morally unrestrained person is the cause of his own evil. He cannot blame it on someone else.† Likewise, the person who is able to exercise self-control is responsible for his own good conduct.

Christian Marriage

Marriage is sanctified only when it meets certain conditions. First, it must be consummated according to the word. Secondly, the marriage union must be submissive to God. Finally, the married couple must live "with a true heart, in full assurance of faith, having hearts that have been showered from an evil conscience, and the body washed with pure water, and holding the confession of hope; for he is faithful that promised." (Heb. 10:22,23)

The happiness of a marriage should never be measured by either wealth or beauty. Instead, it should be measured by moral excellence. As a certain playwright said, "Beauty helps no wife with her husband. But virtue has helped many. For every good wife who is attached to her husband knows how to practice moderation."

The Role Of The Wife Who Knows God

Fittingly, the Scripture has said that woman is given by God as "a help" to man. A husband may have some annoying faults that affect the harmony of the marriage. If so, the wife should try to remedy these annoyances by using good sense and persuasion. But if her husband does not yield, then she should, nevertheless, try to lead a sinless life, to the extent humanly possible. For she realizes that God is her helper and her companion in such a course of conduct. He is her true Defender and her Saviour—in both the present and the future. So she should make God her leader and the guide for all her actions. She should consider sober-mindedness and righteousness her work. Her life's goal is to incur the favor of God. That is so whether it be necessary to die or to live.

Gracefully, the apostle says in the letter to Titus, "The older women should be of godly behavior, not slanderers, not enslaved to much wine. They should counsel the young women to be lovers of their husbands, lovers of their children, discreet, chaste, housekeepers, good, subject to their own husbands; that the word of God is not blasphemed." (Tit. 2:3-5) And, then, as if putting the finishing touch to the matter of marriage, he adds: "Marriage is honorable in all, and the bed undefiled: but God will judge whoremongers and adulterers." (Heb. 13:4)

As far as perfection is concerned, there is the same goal and the same end for both man and woman. Peter speaks equally to both in his letter, saying, "Though now for a season, if need be, you are in heaviness through manifold temptations; that the trial of your faith, being much more precious than that of gold which perishes, though it be tried with fire, might be found unto praise, and honor, and glory at the revelation of Jesus Christ; whom, having not seen, you love; in whom, though now you do not see him, yet believing, you rejoice with unspeakable joy, and full of glory, receiving the end of your faith, the salvation of your souls." (1 Pet. 1:6-9)

21

Searching For Truth

Now I'm going to respond to the objections that the Greeks and Jews make. They say they shouldn't believe [in Christ] because different Christian sects teach conflicting things. For, as they point out, the truth is warped when some teach one set of beliefs and others teach another set.

My response is that quite a few sects have also sprung up among the Jews. And the same is true of the most famous schools of Greek philosophy. Yet the Jews and philosophers don't think anyone should hesitate to become a Jew or a philosopher just because of these conflicting sects. Furthermore, the Lord foretold that heresies would be sown among the truth like "weeds among the wheat." (Matt. 13:24)

And what the Lord predicted must take place. All good things are invariably stained by some foul blot. For example, someone may violate his commitment and leave the faith. Should we forsake the truth simply because he has failed to live up to his beliefs? No, but a good man keeps his promises, even though others may not do so. In the same way, we are obligated to not transgress the rule of the church in any way. We particularly hold to our profession [of Christianity] in those points that are most essential. But the heretics transgress those things. So the Jews and Greeks should believe only those [Christians] who hold firmly to the truth.

To illustrate, physicians hold conflicting opinions. Yet they still all treat patients. If someone is ill and needs treatment, does he refuse to go to the doctor because of the differing schools of medicine? Of course not!' In the same way, he who is sick in soul and who worships idols can't use the existence of heretical sects as an excuse to delay turning to God and receiving treatment for his [soul's] health.

Moreover, it was said that "heresies exist on account of those that are approved." (1 Cor. 11:19) By "approved," [the apostle] means those who apply the teaching of the Lord with discrimination. To illustrate, money-changers are not considered "approved" unless they can distinguish real money from counterfeit.

For this reason, it requires great attention and consideration to investigate how we should live. And to determine what is true righteousness. The very fact that truth is difficult to grasp causes people to ask questions. And from such questions, heresies spring up. (1 Tim. 6:3,4)) The teachers of heresies are those who have not accurately learned or understood. They have only the *semblance* of knowledge. Self-love and vanity are their trademarks.

So the real truth should be examined with great care. Only real truth searches for the true God. But the toil for truth is followed by sweetness of discovery and contemplation.

We must undertake the toil of discovery because of these heresies. And we must never abandon this quest. Suppose someone set before you a bowl of fruit. And suppose some of the fruit was real but the rest was actually made of wax—even though it looked real. Would you refuse to eat either kind of fruit just because it was not easy to tell the two apart? In the same way, [when eating from the bowl of truth], we must distinguish the true from the counterfeit. We do this by exercising understanding through contemplation and by deep reasoning.

To use another illustration, there is only one royal highway. But there are many other types of highways. Some lead to the edge of a cliff. Others lead to a rushing river or to a deep sea. Yet, no one refuses to travel simply because of this diversity of roads. Instead, they make use of the royal road, which is safe and well-traveled. Likewise, though some say one thing about truth, and others say something different, we must not abandon our search. Instead, we must seek out the most accurate knowledge of truth. Just because weeds spring up among garden-grown vegetables, should the gardeners refuse to garden?

Obviously, there are many good examples from nature. From these, we ought to discover the way of truth. So we must accept and obey the truth. And we must distinguish the false, unnatural, hostile, and unseemly, from that which is true. This truth is in accord with nature. It is consistent and seemly. If we don't accept this truth, we are justly condemned.

So the excuse the Greeks make is useless. Those who are willing *shall* find the truth. But those who make unfounded excuses face certain condemnation. I believe that every sincere person will acknowledge the fact that truth *can* be found. Since truth can be demonstrated, it is necessary to answer sincere questions and to demonstrate from the Scriptures the fallacy of various heresies. It is also necessary to show that we can find the most accurate knowledge and the best set of principles only in the truth and in the testimony of the ancient church.

Some who leave the truth deceive only themselves. Others try to deceive their neighbors also. Some are called wise in their own opinions. They think they have found the truth, but they have no real evidence for their belief. They deceive themselves into thinking they have reached a resting place. Many of them avoid investigation for fear they will be discredited. They reject instruction for fear of condemnation. These deceivers are very clever. They are aware that they know nothing, yet they darken the truth with arguments that sound plausible.

However, in my opinion, the very nature of their arguments differs from those that are true. Therefore, heresies should be labeled by the manner in which they differ from the truth. The deceivers teach things for the destruction of men. They bury themselves in human teachings that they themselves invented. They would rather be the head of some heretical school than to [properly] preside over the church.

22

Scripture: The Basis Of Truth

There are many people who are ready to strive after the most excellent pursuits. Such people will not stop searching for truth until they get the proof from the Scriptures themselves. For the Scriptures are the basis of truth.†

To abandon mere human opinion is a great thing. But it is essential to choose accurate knowledge over the false wisdom of human opinion. If you desire eternal rest, you should know that the entrance to it is narrow. And it requires toil to enter it. (Matt. 7:14) When someone receives the Gospel, he should not turn back, like Lot's wife. He should not return to his former life, which clinged to sensual things. Neither should he go back to heresies. "For he that loves father or mother more than me, is not worthy of me." (Matt. 10:37) Those words were spoken by the father and teacher of the truth, who regenerates old things and creates new things. He also nourishes those souls that are chosen. His words mean that those who turn back are unworthy to be a son, disciple, or friend of God. "For no man who puts his hand to the plow, and then looks back, is fit for the kingdom of God." (Luke 9:62)

Even down to our own time, many think that Mary was in the childbearing state on account of the birth of her child. But she was not. For some say that, after she gave birth [to Jesus], she was examined and found to [still] be a virgin.*

The Scriptures of the Lord are like that to us. They gave birth to the truth, but they remain virgin in the concealment of the mysteries of truth. The Scripture says, "And she brought forth; yet she did not bring forth." For she [Mary] conceived by herself, and not from joining with another. Those who know God recognize that the Scriptures have brought forth [truth]. But the heretics, not having learned the Scriptures, dismiss the Scriptures as not giving birth to [truth].

Some men let the Word speak, and they build proofs from it. Others, however, give themselves up to pleasures. They distort Scripture to agree with their lusts. (2 Pet. 3:16) So I think the lover of truth needs force of soul. For those who attempt the greatest things often fail. To succeed, they must follow the rule of truth and cleave to the truth.

He who has rejected the beliefs handed down by the church and has darted off to the opinions of heretical men, has ceased to be a man of God. He is like those mythical men who became beasts after being drugged by Circe. He has ceased to remain faithful to the Lord. But, if upon hearing the Scriptures, he leaves this deception and turns to the truth, then he is like those in the myths who were changed from men into gods.

Christ Teaches Through The Scriptures

The source of our teaching is the Lord. He teaches through the prophets, the Gospel, and the blessed apostles. He teaches us "in various ways and at various times," leading us from the beginning of knowledge to the end. (Heb. 1:1) If anyone should think that another source is necessary, then the true source could no longer be preserved.

He who believes the Scriptures and the voice of the Lord is justly [regarded as] faithful. We use it as the criterion to

---

*Some early Christians believed that Mary remained a virgin her entire life and that Jesus' brothers were sons of Joseph from a prior marriage.

discover [the truth of] things. Things that need to be subjected to examination are not believed until they have been so examined. Anything falling into this category cannot be a "first principle." So logically, the "first principle" surpasses demonstration and must be grasped by faith. At the same time, we abundantly receive demonstrations *in reference* to the first principle. We are thereby trained by the voice of the Lord in the knowledge of the truth.

We should not give our loyalty to men simply on the basis of their bare statements. For tomorrow they might state the opposite of what they're telling us now. So when a statement must be confirmed, we can't confirm it from men's testimony. Instead, we must verify it by the voice of the Lord. For it is the surest of all proofs. In fact, it's the *only* proof.

Those who have merely *tasted* the Scriptures are the ones I call simple "believers." But those who have advanced further and have become accurate teachers of the truth, I designate as "the ones who know God." To illustrate from everyday life, craftsmen are superior to unskilled people. Craftsmen create things that surpass ordinary ideas. Likewise, we can convince others by supplying proof in faith from the Scriptures. We do this by giving a thorough explanation of individual Scripture passages from the rest of the Scriptures themselves.

How Heretics Misuse The Scriptures

Sometimes heretics quote from the prophetic Scriptures, but they misuse them in several ways. First, they don't make use of *all* the Scriptures. Secondly, when they do cite a passage, they don't quote it in its entirety. Thirdly, they quote prophetic statements out of context. Furthermore, they like to select ambiguous passages, so they can distort them to agree with their own opinions. Finally, they gather a few expressions here and there, not looking to the meaning, but making use of the mere words, while altering the meaning.

But truth is not found by twisting the meanings [of Scripture]. Doing violence to the Scriptures is no way to establish one's teachings. Yet, people have used this method to corrupt all true teaching. However, to find truth, a person must consider what perfectly belongs to the Sovereign God and what is becoming to him. One must also establish the meaning of any particular Scripture passage by using other similar passages from Scripture.

In contrast, heretics do not want to turn to the truth. That's because they don't want to abandon the claims that self-love makes on them. When they promote false teachings to men, they are plainly fighting against almost the whole body of Scripture. Those of us who challenge them are constantly proving them to be in error. So they disparage us, saying that we are of a different nature. They say we are unable to understand those things that have been specially [revealed] to them.

However, we overturn their teachings by clearly showing that their doctrines contradict the Scriptures. They then do one of two things: First, they often contradict their own teachings. They sometimes falsely deny that they have taught certain things. So they are ashamed to admit publicly what they pride themselves on teaching in private. When one examines the error of heretical teachings, he finds that this is true of all of them. Secondly, they simply reject the prophecies [of Scripture.] In effect, they reject their only hope. They invariably prefer their teachings over that spoken by the Lord through the prophets and the Gospel, which has been confirmed by the apostles.

Although they read the books [of Scripture] that we have readily at hand, they reject them as useless. In their eagerness to surpass common faith, they have departed from the truth. They go to the height of irreverence—disbelieving the Scriptures themselves. They would rather do this than to be removed from their positions of honor in their heresies and the coveted first seat in their churches. For the same reason, they eagerly embrace the prominent couch of honor in their falsely-called love feasts.

The knowledge of truth among us from what we already believe generates faith in what we do not yet believe. This faith is the essence of proof. But it seems that no heresy is able to hear

Scripture: The Basis Of Truth

what is *worthwhile*, but only what is *pleasurable*. Nevertheless, if any heretic would only obey the truth, he would be healed.

As is true with most illnesses, the cure for pride is threefold. First the cause of pride must be diagnosed. Then the type of treatment must be ascertained. Finally, the soul must be disciplined [to prevent pride from developing again]. When a soul is perverted by unnatural teachings, it is like a diseased eye. Because it cannot clearly see the light of truth, it overlooks the obvious.

They say that eels are caught in muddy water, where they are unable to see. Just as mischievous boys sometimes lock their teacher out of the school building, heretics shut out the prophecies from their church. They regard them with suspicion because of the rebuke and admonition contained in them. They sew together a multitude of lies and illusions. So it looks like they are only acting reasonably in rejecting the Scriptures. They are not righteous because they don't like God's commands. In other words, they don't like the Holy Spirit.

They are like empty almonds.† When people say that an almond is "empty," they don't mean that there is nothing inside. Rather, they mean that the contents are worthless. In the same way, we say that heretics are "empty" because they are devoid of the counsels of God and of the traditions of Christ. Their doctrines are bitter, like the wild almond. For the most part, they create their own teachings, except for certain truths they are unable to discard or hide because the truths are too evident.

23

Medicine For The Soul

In a war, a soldier must not leave the post his commander has assigned him. Likewise, we must not desert the post the Logos has assigned us. For we have received him as the guide of knowledge and life. But most people have never inquired if there is One we ought to follow. They never ask who he is or how he is to be followed. The believer's life must be like the Logos, so as to be able to follow God. For God brings everything from the beginning to the end by the right course.

When a Christian sins against the Logos, he is thereby sinning against God. Sometimes a Christian sins because of a sudden outside influence that has made him powerless. If so, he should be careful to have the influence of sound teaching at hand. But in some cases, the Christian has actually become "ordinary" again, as the Scripture says. This happens when he is regularly overcome by the habits which formerly controlled him. In that case, he must completely stop those habits and discipline his soul to oppose them.

If conflicting teachings draw some away from the faith, these stumbling blocks should be removed. In such a situation, the one who is having doubts should go to a teacher in the church who is skilled at reconciling doctrines. The teacher will be able to explain the truth by showing the link between the two Testaments.* By

---

*The Gnostics generally rejected the Old Testament as being the work of a different God than that of the New Testament.

using the power of the Scriptures he will be able to restore the unsteady who are timid in the faith.

We humans seem to be attracted to ideas based on human opinions, rather than to those based on the truth. This is so even when the human opinions are contradictory. The reason humans reject the truth is that it is morally strict and solemn.

There are three states of the soul: ignorance, opinion, and knowledge. The Gentiles are in the state of ignorance. The heretics are in the state of opinion. They actually despise and laugh at each other. For the same opinion may be honored by some and condemned as insane by others. But the true church is in the state of knowledge. Sensuousness is characteristic of the Gentiles. Quarreling is characteristic of the heretical sects. Joy is characteristic of the church. And ecstasy is characteristic of the one who knows God.

If a person wants to become a poet, he studies Homer, so he can become like Homer. If he wants to become an orator, he studies Demosthenes, so he can become like Demosthenes. Similarly, he who listens to the Lord and follows the prophecy given by him will be formed perfectly in the likeness of the Teacher—becoming divine although walking in the flesh. (2 Pet. 1:4) But those who do not follow God wherever he leads fall from this lofty place. And God leads us in the inspired Scriptures.

Causes Of Sin

Though men's actions are ten thousand in number, there are only two sources of all sin: ignorance and inability. Both of these depend on ourselves. Either we will not *learn,* or we will not *restrain* our lust. If one does not learn, he does not judge well. If he does not restrain his lust, he cannot comply with right judgments. If someone is deceived in his mind, he will be unable to act correctly, even though he is quite capable of doing what he mistakenly knows. Another man may be capable of judging what is required of him, but he will not stay pure if he does not have the *power* to do what is right.

So there are two remedies to sin. The first type of sin needs knowledge and clear proof from the testimony of the Scriptures. The other type of sin needs the training according to the Logos. This training is regulated by the discipline of faith and fear. Both disciplines develop into perfect love. The completeness of the one who knows God is twofold: It is part contemplation of knowledge, and it is part action.

I wish the heretics would learn from these notes, and turn to the sovereign God! But if they, like deaf serpents, will not listen to this new song [of Christianity]—which is really very old—I pray that God will chastise them. I pray that they will receive enough fatherly rebuke *now*—before the Judgment—so they will become ashamed and repent.

How God Disciplines

Partial corrections are called chastisements. Many of us who have been in transgression have incurred this, by falling away from the Lord's people. As children are chastised by their teacher, or by their father, so we are chastised by God. God does not *punish* us, because punishment is retaliation for evil. Rather, God chastises for the good of those in error, whether individually or collectively.

I write these things in order to persuade and lead to the truth those who are not entirely incurable. Some, however, cannot bear to listen to those who urge them to turn to the truth. They ridicule and blaspheme the truth. They claim they have knowledge of the greatest things in the universe, without having learned, inquired, labored, or discovered how to even think straight. But we should have compassion on them rather than hating them for their obstinacy.

If one is curable, let him listen with the ears of his soul. For he is able to bear the frankness of the truth, which cuts away and burns false opinions. But some crave glory. So they use various arguments to willingly evade the things delivered by the blessed apostles and teachers. The things delivered by the apostles are wedded to inspired words. However, heretics establish their false doctrines by using *human* teaching to oppose *divine* tradition.

However, the one who knows God has matured in the Scriptures. He maintains apostolic doctrines and the orthodox teachings of the church. He truly lives in agreement with the gospel. He has discovered the proofs he sought from the Law and the Prophets. His life is nothing but deeds and words corresponding to the tradition of the Lord.

However, the apostle says, "All do not have knowledge. For I would not have you to be ignorant, brothers, that all were under the cloud, and partook of spiritual meat and drink." (1 Cor. 10:1,3,4) He clearly establishes that all who heard the word did not grasp the magnitude of knowledge in speech or deed. Therefore, he added, "He was not well pleased with all of them." (Luke 6:46) Who was not pleased? The same one who said, "Why do you call me Lord, and do not do the will of my Father?" (Matt. 7:21) That is the Savior's teaching, which is spiritual food to us. It is the water of knowing God, which eternally quenches thirst.

> *The one who knows God has matured in the Scriptures.*

Does Knowledge Puff Up?

But someone may say, "Knowledge is said 'to puff up.'" (1 Cor. 8:1) To which I reply, *"Falsely-called* knowledge puffs up." That is, if we suppose the expression means "to be inflated with pride." However, I think the expression of the apostle actually means "to entertain great and true sentiments." This solves the difficulty.

Using the Scriptures, let's establish what has been said. Solomon says, "Wisdom has inflated her children." Does this mean that wisdom inflates with pride?† Of course, not!† The teachings of the Lord do not cause egotism. Instead, they produce trust in the truth. They expand the mind through knowledge revealed in Scripture. They produce contempt for the things that drag us into sin. This is the meaning of the expression, "inflated." It teaches the splendor of wisdom, which is implanted in her children by instruction. The apostle says, "I will not know the speech of those that are puffed up, but the power." (1 Cor. 4:19) The power of the children of wisdom, who are "inflated," lies in correctly understanding the Scriptures. He says, as it were, "I shall know if you rightly entertain great thoughts respecting knowledge."

David says that "God is known in Judea," referring to those who are Israelites according to knowledge. Judea is interpreted "Confession." The apostle stated it correctly, "You shall not commit adultery. You shall not steal. You shall not covet. And if there is any other commandment, it is fulfilled in this command, 'You shall love your neighbor as yourself.'" (Rom. 13:9)

We must never pervert the truth, like those who follow heresies. Nor should we steal the canon of the church by gratifying our own lusts and vanity. Nor do we cheat our neighbors. For it is our duty above all, in showing love to our neighbors, to teach them to cling to the truth. Accordingly, it is clearly said, "Declare among the pagans his statutes." We do this so they will not be judged, but that those who listen will be converted. In this way, they too can come to know God.[†]

24

Caring For Your Neighbor

The one who knows God never holds a grudge against those who have sinned against him. Rather, he forgives them. He prays, "Forgive us, because we also forgive others." (Matt. 6:12) For God commands us to covet nothing and to hate no one. All men are the creation of the same God. Jesus said that the ones who know him are to be perfect as his "heavenly Father [is perfect]." (Matt. 5:48) For it is Jesus himself who says, "Come, children, hear from me the fear of the Lord." (Ps. 34:11) He does not want the one who knows God to stand in need of help from the angels. Rather Jesus wants him to receive it directly from Himself, having become worthy of this.

This kind of man does not merely *request* what he needs from the Lord. He asks for it *boldly*. When he sees his brothers in need, the one who knows God will not ask for wealth to share with them. Instead, he will pray that they receive only what they *need*. This way the man of God gives his prayer to those in need. And by his prayer their needs are supplied, without his knowledge, and without vanity on his part.

God often sends poverty, disease, and other similar trials on people as discipline for their past conduct and as instruction for their future conduct. Still, the one who knows God can ask God to relieve [others] from these trials. He brings kindness to others, having become the instrument of God's goodness.

It is said that the apostle Matthew used to constantly preach, "If a Christian's neighbor sins, the Christian himself has sinned. For if he had conducted himself as the Word says, his neighbor would have been filled with such reverence for the Christian life that he would not sin any longer."

So what shall we say about the one who knows God? The apostle asks, "Don't you know that you are the temple of God?" (1 Cor. 3:16) So the one who knows God partakes of divinity. (2 Pet. 1:4) He is already holy. He carries God in his body, and God carries him. The Scripture shows that sinning is foreign to him, saying, "Do not look on a strange woman with lust." (Matt. 5:28) This plainly demonstrates that sin is foreign and contrary to the nature of the temple of God. The temple is both great and small. It is as great as the [whole] church. And it is as small as the individual man who preserves the seed of Abraham. He then who has God dwelling in him will not desire anything else. By putting away all hindrances and distractions, he opens the heavens through knowledge. He passes through the spiritual entities, past all rule and authority, and touches the highest thrones themselves.

Like mixing 'a serpent with a dove,' (Matt. 10:16), the one who knows God combines faith with hope. He lives perfectly, with a good conscience. He does this to gain the future for which he has hoped. He is aware of the blessing he has been given, having become worthy to receive it. He is moved from slavery to adoption as a result of knowing God. Or, I should say, because he is known by God. To obtain this end, he has put forth energies corresponding to the worth of grace. For works follow knowledge just as the shadow follows the body.

He is not agitated by anything that happens. And he doesn't question the things which take place by divine arrangement for the good. Furthermore, he is not reluctant to die. For he has a good conscience and is prepared to be seen by the Powers. Being cleansed from all the stains of the soul, he is certain that it will be better with him after his departure [from this life].

So he never prefers pleasure and profit to the divine arrangement. He trains himself by the commandments so he will please the Lord in all things. He trains so he will be blameless before the world, since all things depend on the one sovereign God. It is written that the Son of God came to his own, and his own did not receive him. So in the use of worldly things, he gives thanks and he praises the creation. He also is praised for using them correctly.

Through knowledge, he has stored food for thought. Because he has nobly embraced the greatness of knowledge, he advances to the holy reward of being carried from this life. He has heard the Psalm which says, "Encircle Zion and surround it. Count its towers." (Ps. 48:12) This implies, I believe, that those who have sublimely embraced the Word and become like lofty towers will stand firmly in faith and knowledge.

Conclusion

These statements about knowing God contain the seeds of this matter, presented in as concise a way as possible. Let them be shared with the Greeks. It should be understood, however, that although the one who is a mere believer may follow one or two of these things, he will invariably be found to not be following all of them. And what he does follow will not be done with the highest understanding. For these can only be done by the one who knows God.

Appendix

The chapter designations used in this book are those of the modern editor. In the translation of William Wilson, which was the basis of this rendition, the chapters are numbered differently. The chapter designations used in this book correlate to those of Mr. Wilson as follows:

Chapter Designation Here	Wilson Translation
Part One	*Who Is The Rich Man?*
1	1-3
2	4-9
3	10-15
4	16-19
5	20-27a
6	27b-33
7	34-38
8	39-42
Part Two	*Miscellanies*
9	Bk. 2, ch. 20 (excerpts)
10	Bk. 7, ch. 12a
11	Bk. 7, ch. 12b
12	Bk. 7, ch. 7a
13	Bk. 7, ch. 7b
14	Bk. 2, ch. 19a
15	Bk. 2, ch. 6
16	Bk. 4, ch. 18
17	Bk. 7, ch. 11
18	Bk. 7, ch. 8,14a
19	Bk. 7, ch. 14b
20	Bk. 4, ch. 19,20 (excerpts)
21	Bk. 7, ch. 15
22	Bk. 7, ch. 16a
23	Bk. 7, ch. 16b
24	Bk. 7, ch. 13

It should be noted that chapter 9 herein is composed only of excerpts from book 2, chapter 20 of the *Miscellanies*. Similarly, the first half of chapter 20 herein is composed only of excerpts from book 4, chapter 19 of the *Miscellanies*.

The following repetitive or unclear sentences and clauses were omitted from the main text. None of these statements have any doctrinal significance that we can perceive.

From Part One
(Who Is The Rich Man That Shall Be Saved?)

Chap. 3 (*Rich Man*, Ch. 10-15)

The tendency to indulge the passions produces its own effects. It strangles our reason, pressing it down and inflaming it with its inbred lusts.

Chap. 4 (*Rich Man*, Ch. 16-19)

So it is clear that by being poor in those things, by riches of which one destroys it, it is saved, and by being rich in those things, riches of which ruin it, it is killed. ...Not one who could not live rich. ...We know that riches and the "treasure" mentioned in our Lord's words are not necessarily different.

Chap. 5 (*Rich Man*, Ch. 20-27a)

They don't even come close to doing so. ...You may even go against wealth. ...So let the camel, which goes through a narrow and tight way in front of the rich man, symbolize something loftier. (I have explained this mystery of the Savior in my previous work, "Exposition of the First Principles and of Theology.")

Chap. 7 (*Rich Man*, Ch. 34-38)

He reckons the whole as his. ...For there is the uncertainty of ignorance. ..Not to touch your flesh, but to speak to the King of eternity dwelling in you. ...For let not this be left to despondency and despair by you, if you learn who the rich man is that has not a place in heaven, and what way he uses his property.

Chap. 8 (*Rich Man*, Ch. 39-42)

Also, is what in each case the end of all cries aloud. ...If you are unmoved by bold speech, then your soul is blinded by melting away. ...and the disciples of God, and God, who is surety.

From Part Two
(Miscellanies)

Chap. 10 (*Misc.*, Bk. 7, Ch. 12a):

Let these things, then, be so. ...Caring then for himself alone, he is surpassed by him who is inferior, as far as his own personal salvation is concerned, but who is superior in the conduct of life, preserving certainly, in his care for the truth, a minute image. ...The one who knows God, because of his surpassing holiness, is better prepared to fail to get what he asks, than to get when he does not ask. ...Even though they were [originally] given by God. ...so far, that is, as is necessary. ...For the one [day of the week] has its name from Hermes, and the other from Aphrodite. ...We have already shown above the three varieties of fornication, according to the apostle: love of pleasure, love of money, and idolatry.

Chap. 11 (*Misc.*, Bk. 7, Ch. 12b):

So that the place may not compel him, but his mode of life show him to be just. ...This is preceded by the reception of knowledge. ...Since there is not equal love in "having sown the flesh" and in having formed the soul for knowledge. . .And so these are to him, friends. ...But the one who knows God is cautious in accommodation, lest he be not perceived, or lest the accommodation become disposition.

Chap. 12 (*Misc.*, Bk. 7, Ch. 7a):

The prophet obviously spoke wisely when he said, "Kindness, instruction and knowledge teach me" [Ps. 119:66], magnifying the supremacy of perfection by a climax. ...He also gives thanks for his use of it by the Logos given to him. ...But the sensitivity of the air, the intensely keen perception of the angels and the power which reaches the soul's consciousness know all things at the very moment of thought, by awesome power and without the physical sensation of hearing. ...He has this fellowship through knowledge, life and thanksgiving. ...When he makes these offerings, he does so acknowledging his thanks for the gift. ...

No man desires a drink, but to actually drink something drinkable, and no man desires an inheritance, but to actually inherit. Likewise, no man desires merely knowledge, but to actually know. Or a right government, but to take part in the government. So, the subjects of our prayers are the subjects of our requests, and the subjects of requests are the objects of our desires. Therefore, prayer always follows desire, with the view of having the blessings and advantages offered ..

For he is such by possession. ...Whence, as is right, there being only one good God, that some good things be given from him alone, and that some remain, we and the angels pray. But not similarly. For it is not the same thing to pray that the gift remain, and to endeavor to obtain it for the first time. ...It follows the eagerness of the spirit directed towards the intellectual essence. ...The followers of Prodicus, in particular, are the ones who teach this. Just so they don't get swelled heads about this godless wisdom of theirs, as though it was something original, let me point out that a group of philosophers called the Cyrenaics embraced this doctrine before. At any rate, the unholy "knowledge" of those who are mistaken as truly knowing God will be proven false in due time. We won't go into an assault on their doctrines right now, since the subject we are on at the moment. ...

Without doubt, the holiness of the one who truly knows God, in union with God, is demonstrated by his voluntary confession of the perfect kindness of God. For the holiness of the one who knows God and the responding kindness of the friend of God are a kind of interactive movement of God's benevolent guidance. . .As one who knows God, he is associated with intellectual and spiritual objects.

Chap. 13 (*Misc.*, Bk. 7, Ch. 7b):

...Need and shortcoming are measured with reference to what relates to each person. So if a person has wisdom, and wisdom is a divine thing, then he who partakes of what lacks nothing will himself lack nothing. Wisdom is not given out by activity and receptivity moving and stopping each other, or by anything being abstracted or becoming defective. Therefore activity remains undiminished in the act of communication. ...This advancement is through progressive stages and acts of administration. ...He exhorts some people, and helps others who of themselves have become worthy. ...So the promise is accomplished. ...That is, in the direction of learning, and training, and well-doing, and pleasing God. ...And God expects of us the things which pertain to us, both present and absent, the choice, and desire, and possession, and use, and permanence. ...He is engaged in contemplation which has everlasting remembrance.

Chap. 14 (*Misc.*, Bk. 2, Ch. 19a):

He is restored from what he was, and the whole is named from a part.

Chap. 15 (*Misc.*, Bk. 2, chap. 6):

Some choose easily, others repent of their sins, still others reflect on their failures, then repent. ...This is so whether faith is based on love or only on fear (as critics claim). ..."Lord, who has believed our report?" Isaiah asks. ...We do not yet understand that the word of the Lord involves demonstration. ...The amber teardrop drags twigs to itself, and the lump sets chaff in motion. And the substances attracted obey them, influenced by a subtle spirit, not as a cause, but as a concurring cause. ...There are even two types of vice. One involves cunning and secrecy, the

Appendix

other involves leading and driving with violence. In each example, the drawing of the one and the receptivity of the other are essential .

Basilides' followers say faith is the soul's consent to things which cannot be seen. .. God's Word declares that He is faithful. If to believe is to assume the source is trustworthy, how can philosophers think that what proceeds from themselves is true? Agreeing with something you have seen is not assumption, but rather acknowledging something certain. Who is more powerful than God? Unbelief is the weak theory of someone opposed to God. It is not easy for a skeptical person to have faith. Faith is a decision to believe something before all the facts are known. Confidence is a strong judgment about something. ...

"The just shall live by faith" speaks of both the covenant and the commandments. These, being separate things, are one in power and are dispensed through the Son by one God. ..Fear, the instructor of the law, is considered to be fear by those who believe in it. For if its existence is shown in what it does, it is assumed to be present whether or not it is working and present. It does not itself create faith, but is by faith tested and proved accurate. Such a change from unbelief to faith is divine.

Chap. 16 (*Misc.*, Bk. 4, ch. 18):

The latter is twofold, unwritten and written. ...He means, if I do not testify from a disposition determined by the love of one who knows God. ...Likewise, even if I cast away fleshly desires [but have not love]. ...This is in comparison to him who testifies as one who knows God, and the crowd, and being reckoned nothing better. ...like as Christ, that is the presence of the Lord who loves us; and our loving teaching of, and discipline according to Christ. ...And it makes a difference whether it is wrought by faith or by knowledge. ...Nor has the likes of this reward entered into the heart of man. . .For a dream is part physical and part imagination. ...She said that in this way she had satisfied the lover's desire. .The soul is in agreement with whatever vision a person dreams about. So when one looks with lust, it's as though he were dreaming while still awake. ...

Exhibiting the sacred symbol, the bright impress of righteousness to the angels that wait on the ascension. I mean the unction of acceptance, the quality of disposition which resides in the soul that is gladdened by the communication of the Holy Spirit. This glory, which shone forth on the face of Moses, the people could not look on. Wherefore he took a veil for the glory, to those who looked carnally. For those, who demand toll, detain those who bring in any worldly things, who are burdened with their own passions. But he who is free of all things which are subject to duty, and is full of knowledge, and of the righteousness of works, they pass on with their good wishes, blessing the man with his work. "And his life shall not fall away"—the leaf of the living tree that is nourished "by the water-courses." Now the righteous are likened to fruit-bearing trees, and not only to such as are of the nature of tall-growing ones. And in the sacrificial oblations, according to the law, there were those who looked for blemishes in the sacrifices. They who are skilled in such matters distinguish propension from lust; and assign the latter, as being irrational, to pleasures and licentiousness; and propension, as being a rational movement, they assign to the necessities of nature.

Chap. 17 (*Misc.*, Bk. 7, Ch. 11):

This begins with admiration of Creation itself. ...Through the power of impulse thence derived. ...And this is to become worthy of speculation, of such a character, and such importance. ...Training himself in knowledge, he exercises himself in larger generalizations and grander propositions. ...The Lord acts through man's mouth. He also assumed flesh. .But in sensation he is not the primary subject of it. ...These things are already known, being hoped for so as to be apprehended. ...He has everything dependent on himself for the attainment of the end. ...

Something can be caused through foolishness and the cooperation of the devil. But that doesn't mean that the act itself is foolishness or is the devil. In the same way, no action is wisdom. Wisdom is a state of mind, and no action is a state of mind. The action coming from ignorance is not ignorance, but only an evil action brought through ignorance. ...Neither agitations of mind nor sins are corruption, though they proceed from corruption. ...I know not how (for it is right to use mild language). ...As they say, adamant is by fire. ...Further, agreement on the same thing is consent. ...Friendship is fulfilled in likeness; the community lying in oneness. ...These are titles of nobility, knowledge, and perfection in the contemplation of God.

Chap. 18 (*Misc.*, Bk. 7, Ch. 8, 14a):

If it is the judgment of one who does and says things that has the potential to be wrong, not the suffering of the one who is wronged. ...You seek to deprive at least as to your involvement with these qualities.

Chap. 19 (*Misc.*, Bk. 7, Ch. 14b):

The one who knows God will accomplish this either by greatness of mind or by imitation of what is better. That is a third cause. "Forgive and you shall be forgiven." This commandment brings us to salvation through the superabundance of goodness. ...Let this example be sufficient for those who have ears. For it is not required to unfold the mystery, but only to indicate what is sufficient for those who are partakers in knowledge to bring it to mind. ...

If, then, the statement being elliptical, we understand what is wanting, in order to complete the section for those who are incapable of understanding what is left out, we shall both know the will of God, and shall walk at once piously and magnanimously, as befits the dignity of the commandment.

Chap. 20 (*Misc.*, Bk. 4, ch. 20):

It was not only Moses who heard God say, "I have spoken to you once, and twice, saying, 'I have seen this people, and look, they are stiff-necked.' Allow me to exterminate them, and blot out their name from under heaven. And I will make you into a great and wonderful nation much greater than this." [Ex. 32:9,10] But Moses did not answer out of regard for himself, but for the common salvation [of all]: "By no means, oh Lord. Forgive this people their sin, or else blot me out of the book of the living." [Ex. 32:32] How great was Moses' perfection! He preferred to die together with the people than to be saved alone. ...People can suppress external things by waging war against them.

The woman who, with propriety, loves her husband, Euripides describes, while admonishing: "That when her husband says aught/She ought to regard him as speaking well if she say nothing;/And if she will say anything, to do her endeavor to gratify her husband." And again he subjoins the like: "And that the wife should sweetly look sad with her husband,/Should aught evil befall him,/And have in common a share of sorrow and joy." Then, describing her as gentle and kind even in misfortunes, he adds: "And I, when you are ill, will, sharing your sickness, bear it;/And I will bear my share in your misfortunes." And: "Nothing is bitter to me,/For with friends one ought to be happy,/For what else is friendship but this?"

Then, as giving admonitions, he says: "First, then, this is incumbent on her who is endowed with mind, that even if her husband is ugly, he must appear good-looking. For it is for the mind, not the eye, to judge." And so forth. ...All this should be done in accordance with reason. ...Rather, he says, "Follow peace with all men, and holiness, without which no man shall see the Lord. Looking diligently, lest there be any fornicator or profane person, as Esau, who for one morsel surrendered his birthright; and lest any root of bitterness springing up trouble you, and there many be defiled." ...Similarly, Paul also rejoices for Christ's sake that he was "in labors more abundantly, in stripes above measure, in deaths often."

Chap. 21 (*Misc.*, Bk. 7, ch. 15):

Since, in some of the questions previously discussed, the sects also who adhere to other teaching give their help, it will be well first to clear away the obstacles before us. And then, prepared thus for the solution of the difficulties, to advance to the succeeding Miscellany. ...Or those who have already become approved both in life and knowledge. ...And these means must be employed in order to attain to the knowledge of the real truth. ...For whether do they deny or admit that there is such a thing as demonstration?

Chap. 22 (*Misc.*, Bk. 7, Ch. 16a):

What methods of minds and reason should we use to distinguish between true and false propositions? Some criteria are common to all men—such as the five senses. Other criteria belong to those who have set their wills and energies to pursue what is true. ...

Even in the very hour in which he has come to the knowledge of salvation. ...For they form the character, not knowing the true God. ...Now all men have the same judgment. ...But such people, in consequence of falling away from the right path, err in most individual points; as you might expect from not having the faculty for judging of what is true and false, strictly trained to select what is essential. For if they had, they would have obeyed the Scriptures. By his voice and by Scripture, the Lord acts to the benefiting of men. ...But it is not enough merely to state the opinion. ...You will note that when they do quote passages, they make use of words alone. ...Neither knowing, as they affirm, nor using the quotations they adduce, according to their true nature. ...For the rest, even now partly they hold out against admitting the prophetic Scriptures.

Seeing, therefore, the danger that they are in (not in respect of one dogma, but in reference to the maintenance of the heresies) of not discovering the truth. ...For, in consequence of not learning the mysteries of ecclesiastical knowledge, and not having capacity for the grandeur of the truth, too indolent to descend to the bottom of things, reading superficially, they have dismissed the Scriptures. Elated, then, by vain opinion, they are incessantly wrangling, and plainly care more to seem than to be philosophers. Not laying as foundations the necessary first principles of things; and influenced by human opinions, then making the end to suit them, by compulsion; on account of being confuted, they spar with those who are engaged in the prosecution of the true philosophy, and undergo everything, and, as they say, ply every oar. ...And the soul must be accustomed to assume a right attitude to the judgments come to.

Chap. 23 (*Misc.*, Bk. 7, Ch. 16b):

...Nothing, then, can be more clearly seen than those, who know, making affirmations about what they know, and the others respecting what they hold on the strength of opinion, as far as respects affirmation without proof. ...And as, if one devote himself to Ischomachus, he will become a farmer; and to Lampis, a mariner; and to Charidemus, a military commander; and to Simon, an equestrian; and to Perdices, a trader; and to Crobylus, a cook; and to Archelaus, a dancer; and to Homer, a poet; and to Pyrrho, a wrangler; and to Demosthenes, an orator; and to Chrysippus, a dialectician; and to Aristotle, a naturalist; and to Plato, a philosopher.

They will precipitate themselves into judgment. ...I have given these explanations from a wish to discourage those who are eager to learn from the tendency to fall into heresies. I want to keep them from superficial ignorance, stupidity, bad traits, or whatever it should be called. ...

And this will be the case, unless, through the propensity to sloth, they push truth away, or through the desire of fame, endeavor to invent novelties. For those are slothful who, having it in their power to provide themselves with proper proofs for the divine Scriptures from the Scriptures themselves, select only what contributes to their own pleasures. ...For, in truth, what remained to be said—in ecclesiastical knowledge I mean—by such men, Marcion, for example, or Prodicus, and such like, who did not walk in the right way? For they could not have surpassed their predecessors in wisdom, so as to discover anything in addition to what had been uttered by them; for they would have been satisfied had they been able to learn the things laid down before.

He is sent forth by the Lord. ...That is, if you understand the Scriptures magnanimously (which means truly; for nothing is greater than truth). ...But those who speak treacherously with their tongues have the penalties that are on record.

Ch. 24 *(Misc.,* Bk. 7, ch. 13):

He wants him to have protection from himself by obedience. ...He asks in virtue of possessing the prerogative of knowledge, not out of vainglory. .. It sells those who have fallen away to strangers. ...He hastens to that alone for the sake of which alone he knew. ...Since the end he has in view terminates in contemplation by activity of one who knows God in accordance with the commandments.

Index

Abraham, 56, 82, 83
Angels, 66, 77
Apostles, 60, 62, 120

Banquets, 70
Baptism, 45, 48
Barnabas, Letter of, 87

Celibacy, 60, 61
Children, teaching, 68
Church: holding orthodox Christianity, 72, 112, 114, 120, 121; obedience to, 110
Clement of Alexandria: biographical information, 3-5; view of philosophy, 4, 5, 20
Clement of Rome, Letter to Corinthians, 88
Co-laboring with God, 29, 30, 76-80
Conversion, true, 46
Cross, our bearing, 55

Daniel, 56
Death, 60, 66
Demonic forces, 56

Demons, casting out, 41
Discipline from God, 93, 120, 123
Domitian, 48
Dreams, purity in, 65, 66, 70

Elders, appointment of, 48
Entertainment, avoiding wordly, 63, 70
Ephesus, John's residence, 48
Esther, 106
Evangelism, 56, 73, 122

Faith, 66, 84-87, 94, 95
Fasting, 50, 63
Father, God the, 15, 16, 35, 42, 43, 73
Fellowship with God, 69, 70, 72, 80
Foreknowledge, 15, 62, 74
Forgiving others, 103, 123
Free will, 18, 22, 29, 50, 51, 62, 73

Gentiles, inheriting the promises of Israel, 86

Giving alms, 38-40, 58, 65, 66-68, 80, 81
Gnostics, 5, 86, 118
Gospels, Four, 14
Grace, 18, 24, 29, 31, 124
Greeks, 110, 112

Healing, 41
Heretics, 72, 110-112, 114, 120; twisting Scriptures, 115-117
Holiness, 68, 71, 76-80, 104
Holy Spirit, 29, 48, 51, 56, 75, 95
Hymns, 70, 71, 80

Imitation of God and Christ, 81, 94

Jesus, 15, 43, 50, 51, 69; divinity, 15, 42; begotten of the Father, 42, 43
Jews, 110
Job, 56, 68
John, Apostle, 47-50
Joseph, 92, 93
Joy, 68
Judith, 106

Kingdom of heaven, 24, 25, 30, 50

Law, Mosaic, 16-18, 36
Lawsuits, 31, 100-102

Logos, 69, 118
Lord's day, use of term, 63, 64
Love feasts, 116
Love: of fellowman, 35-37, 43, 44, 88-91; of God, 36, 37; of enemies, 58, 59, 63, 101, 102, 123
Lust, 90, 91
Lying, 99, 100

Mammon, meaning of term, 60, 61
Mark, 14
Marriage, 60, 66, 94, 107, 108
Martha, 19
Martyrdom, 62, 95, 96
Mary, 113, 114
Matthew, 21, 124
Meals, reading Scriptures before, 80
Meditation, 76
Mentor, need for, 47
Miriam, 106
Moderation, 59

Nonresistance, 26, 30, 31

Oaths, Christians avoid, 99, 100
Obedience: to God, 35, 37, 43, 46, 66, 85, 104; to church leadership, 73

Index

Overseers, 48

Parents, hating: meaning of phrase, 30, 31, 67
Perfection, Christian, 18, 30, 59, 100, 103-105
Perfume, 70
Persecution, 32, 33, 58, 95, 96, 100
Perseverance, need for, 56
Peter: foremost apostle, 30, 32; his wife, 94
Philosophers, 20, 71, 94, 110
Plato, 83
Pleasure, abstention from worldly, 57, 59, 60, 63, 67, 70, 76
Poor in spirit, meaning of phrase, 24, 25, 27
Poverty, 24, 25, 27, 32, 95
Power, from God, 29, 42, 79
Praise, 70
Prayer: heretics say unnecessary, 72, 73; in general, 50, 61, 62, 66, 67, 69-80; inaudible, 71, 72, 74; intercessory, 41, 47, 62, 123; no need for lengthy, 80; reveals our character, 74; should not be showy, 80
Presence of God, 69, 70, 72, 80
Providence, God's, 77

Ransom, 31, 43
Repentance, 44-51, 81, 85
Resurrection, 50
Retaliation, forbidden to Christians, 103
Return of Christ, 89
Rewards, after death, 62, 89, 94, 96
Rulership, rejection of earthly, 66

Salvation: requirements for, 10-12, 18, 26, 29, 34, 39, 47, 50, 61, 73, 79, 85, 87; losing, 56, 77, 78, 113; role of obedience (works), 10-12, 30, 37, 79, 124
Sanctification, 103, 104
Scripture: the basis of truth, 112-120; heretics twist, 115, 116; interpretation of, 116
Secular employment, 63, 65
Self-discipline, 60, 76
Separation from the world, 55, 58-61, 64, 66, 67, 71, 94, 104
Sickness, 95
Sin: causes of, 119; foreign to Christian, 124; overcoming, 118-120
Smyrna, 48
Sojourners, Christians are, 65

Soul, 20, 22, 24, 26, 51, 56, 57, 60, 64, 75, 97
Spiritual warfare, 55, 56
Stoics, 71
Susanna, 106
Swearing, Christians avoid, 99, 100

Temptation, 62, 63
Testaments, Old and New (use of terms), 118
Theater, 70
Torture, 100
Truth, seeking, 112

Union with God, 40, 67, 75, 104

War, 55
Wealth, Christian view of, 9-53, 66
Widows, 41, 61
Wines, 70
Wives, subjection to husbands, 107
Women, serving God, 106-109

Zaccheus, 21

Will The Real Heretics Please Stand Up

By David W. Bercot

The work you have just read has given you a sample of early Christian thought. Would you like to learn more about the early Christians? If so, we recommend *Will the Real Heretics Please Stand Up*. It's written in a free-flowing readable style, combined with sound scholarship. This 192 page book provides a broad overview of the early Christians—who they were, how they lived, and what they believed. It also explains how the Christianity of that time was lost. Finally, this eye-opening book calls today's church to return to the simple holiness, unfailing love, and patient cross-bearing of the early Christians.

Available at quality Christian bookstores

Or order directly from Scroll Publishing Co., Rt. 19, Box 890, Suite 211, Tyler, TX 75706. Simply enclose $6.95, plus $1.00 for shipping and handling, for each copy. Your copy will be shipped to you within 24 hours of receiving your request.

For a free catalog of early Christian writings and other historical works of interest to Christian seekers, please write Scroll Publishing Co. at the address shown above.

We Don't Speak Great Things—We Live Them

By Mark Felix and Justin Martyr

When a second-century pagan ridiculed Christians for their lack of education, one Christian replied, "We don't speak great things—we *live* them!" That was the essence of early Christianity. It was not a Christianity of words, but of holy, obedient living.

We Don't Speak Great Things—We Live Them contains two second-century Christian works, translated into readable contemporary English: Mark Felix's *Octavius* and Justin Martyr's *First Apology*. They describe the dynamic, living church of the second century and discuss what Christians in that age believed.

The *First Apology* of Justin Martyr is the oldest Christian apology still in existence. Justin penned this work at the risk of his own life. Apart from the inspired New Testament writings, this apology is perhaps the single most valuable work of early Christianity. By means of it, we can look through a window in time to see what Christianity was like at the close of the apostolic age. For example, Justin takes us on a tour of a Christian baptism and a typical Sunday morning church service.

Octavius, written by a Christian lawyer named Mark Felix, takes a look at Christianity from both the pagan and Christian viewpoints. It's not only one of the most readable early Christian works, but it's also a true work of literature. In the end, *Octavius* is more than a challenge to the pagan Romans—it's a challenge to the modern church as well.

Available at quality Christian bookstores

Or order directly from Scroll Publishing Co., Rt. 19, Box 890, Suite 211, Tyler, TX 75706. Simply enclose $6.95, plus $1.00 for shipping and handling, for each copy. Your copy will be shipped to you within 24 hours of receiving your request.